QUESTIONS
AND ANSWERS
—— ON ——
CONVERSION
TO JUDAISM

QUESTIONS AND ANSWERS
—— ON ——
CONVERSION TO JUDAISM

LAWRENCE J. EPSTEIN

JASON ARONSON INC.
Northvale, New Jersey
Jerusalem

This book was set in 12 pt. Berkeley Book by Alpha Graphics of Pittsfield, New Hampshire.

10   9   8   7   6   5   4   3   2   1

Library of Congress Cataloging-in-Publication Data
Epstein, Lawrence J. (Lawrence Jeffrey)
    Questions and answers on conversion to Judaism / by Lawrence J.
  Epstein.
        p.   cm.
    Includes index.
    ISBN 0-7657-5996-9 (alk. paper)
    1. Proselytes and proselyting, Jewish.   I. Title.
BM729.P7E665 1998
296.7'14—dc21   97-44900
                                            CIP

Manufactured in the United States of America. Jason Aronson Inc. offers books and cassettes. For information and catalog write to Jason Aronson Inc., 230 Livingston Street, Northvale, New Jersey 07647 1731. Or visit our website: http://www.aronson.com

This book
is dedicated to Sharon,
a true woman of valor.

Contents

2   REASONS FOR CONVERSION

3   THINKING ABOUT CONVERSION

4   ASKING SOMEONE TO CONSIDER CONVERSION

5 GETTING INFORMATION AND ADVICE
ABOUT CONVERSION AND JUDAISM

6 JUDAISM AND CHRISTIANITY

7 THE CONVERSION PROCESS

II AFTER THE CONVERSION

8 THE EMOTIONAL ASPECTS OF CONVERSION

9 CONFLICT AND CONVERSION

10 CHILDREN AND CONVERSION

Acknowledgments

This is my fourth book on the subject of conversion to Judaism. With each succeeding book, the intellectual and practical debts I owe grow ever higher. It has been a real pleasure to work with so many wonderful people on so interesting and so important a subject.

Arthur Kurzweil of Jason Aronson Inc., a true friend, has, from the start, encouraged my writing efforts. Arthur can recognize when an author's ideas meet an audience's desire for information, and he knows how to encourage and nurture those ideas.

I am grateful for the opportunity to have spoken to an incredible number of gifted people on the subject of conversion to Judaism. In particular, I can identify significant contributions to my thinking from talks with Rabbi Howard Buechler, Rabbi Adam Fisher, Dr. Edward Hoffman, Rabbi Howard Hoffman, Rabbi Jan Kaufman, Rabbi Jay Lapidus, Susan Lustig, Dr. Egon Mayer, Rabbi Steven Moss, Barbara and Julius Shair, and Rabbi Alan Silverstein.

It has been a pleasure to be in contact with many other rabbis and intellectuals in the Jewish community. I have also had a chance, recently most extensively via e-mail, to correspond with hundreds of converts and conversion candidates. In particular, since I began the Conversion to Judaism Home Page

<http://www.convert.org> on the World Wide Web, I have been in contact with an incredibly large number of people interested in the subject of conversion to Judaism. I have been grateful for the kind comments of people around the world, and have learned much from their probing questions and often moving testimonies. It was, in fact, the questions that emerged during many of those e-mail conversations that prompted me to write this book. I began tentative answers on my web site, which I have used, sometimes with expansion and modification, in this work. I am grateful for all those questions; I did not and do not always know the answers, but perhaps just raising some of the issues helps in making people feel less isolated, less concerned that they are the only ones with such feelings.

Tangible support for my efforts came from Barbara and Julius Shair, Florence Melton, Ash Gerecht, and Dick Hazelett. I thank each of them deeply.

I've also received an incredible amount of support from my colleagues at the Suffolk Jewish Communal Planning Council. During my recent tenure as president, the Council produced hundreds of pamphlets on conversion, and distributed them to almost every state and many countries overseas.

In the area of conversion to Judaism, it is vital to keep up with current literature. I appreciate the excellent work being done by writers in this field. Many librarians have been helpful in my efforts to read as much as I can about conversion, and the librarians at Suffolk Community College in particular deserve special mention. They are unfailingly gracious and eager to seek out the required materials, some of which are difficult to locate. Many other people have helped with obtaining materials. Rabbi Carl Perkins, Rabbi Harold Schulweis, and Rabbi Neal Weinberg all forwarded information to me. I would also like to thank all the librarians and researchers who have responded to inter-library loan requests over the years.

Finally, of course, I want to thank my friends and family. Mike Fitzpatrick and Doug Rathgeb, in particular, were always available for talk and help.

My wife Sharon and our children, Michael, Elana, Rachel, and Lisa, are by now almost used to the late-night calls, the unusual faxes, and the long conversations. They provide help when it is needed, solace when necessary, and diversion to complement the work I do each day. The book's dedication to Sharon is a small attempt to thank her.

In the area of conversion to Judaism there are a particularly large number of divergent opinions and strongly held views. Many areas I discuss are controversial. I strongly encourage people who read this book not to take my responses to questions as definitive but as suggestive. I invite those readers to seek out others who have answers, particularly rabbis. I offer this book to provide help, but I know that my own limitations present restrictions concerning the quality and extent of my answers. I am, of course, responsible for these answers. The various sources of encouragement and help that I have enumerated do not constitute any individual's endorsement for the materials contained in this book.

Finally, I want to thank the Conversion to Judaism Resource Center for permission to reprint material from my web site, the Conversion to Judaism Home Page, © 1996 Lawrence J. Epstein.

Introduction

People who are thinking about becoming Jewish understandably have a large number of questions. Born Jews, who are welcoming large numbers of converts for the first time in 1,500 years or more, also have questions about conversion. Jewish educators, professionals in Jewish communal life, intellectuals who think about Jewish life, and all those interested in the Jewish present and Jewish future are, with increasing frequency, facing issues dealing with conversion to Judaism.

In this book, I attempt to respond to questions about conversion in as clear and coherent a way as I can. The emphasis is on the practical. The principal audience for the book is meant to be those who are considering becoming Jewish and want one book in which most if not all of their initial questions will be answered. If this book succeeds, those people will want to learn more. They will want to read more books about Judaism, study with a rabbi, take courses, and so on. Additionally, the book is aimed at those who have joined the Jewish people and all other Jews who are interested in having a handy single-volume reference work.

I am particularly concerned that the responses in this book are incomplete. Many of the issues I discuss are dependent on the particular circumstances of the person asking the question. Therefore, the general answers I give need to be supplemented with reading and authoritative advice from rabbis.

Having said this, I hope that the information and advice contained in these pages will be a useful beginning.

Many people have asked me why I became interested in conversion to Judaism, since neither I, nor my wife, nor our ancestors as far as we can trace them, are converts. That is, I have nothing emotionally or personally at stake in the various discussions about conversion. Yet, in some ways I do. Since I began working in this area I have met, spoken with, or had correspondence with untold numbers of people who embraced Judaism, perhaps 200 rabbis who work with conversion candidates, and other leaders in the Jewish community. By now, I do feel emotionally involved because I am convinced that encouraging conversion and welcoming converts helps many people on a spiritual search and is of extraordinary value to the Jewish community.

I was surprised when I first began reading about conversion to Judaism to discover just how prized it has been in Jewish thought and how widely practiced it has been at certain times in Jewish history. I was struck by how converts could help contemporary American Jewry. In part, that help would be practical. Converts radically transform intermarriages into Jewish marriages. They add to Jewish numbers. They contribute to Jewish charities and raise their children in Jewish homes and schools. These practical factors have been superceded in my own view by that of personal qualities: those who have joined the Jewish people are profoundly good, honest searchers. They have the capacity to do nothing less than reawaken religious sensibilities in a too-secular Jewish population. It is time for the Jewish community to recognize the achievements that converts have made and develop institutional structures that can welcome even more converts.

For me, then, conversion work has become a personal activity. Perhaps I feel emotionally attached to those who convert because, while I was born Jewish, my own Jewish identity and education were tenuous until I was a young adult and chose to learn more about my heritage. I "converted" in a loose sense to my own Judaism.

Finally, though, these practical and emotional reasons for supporting conversion to Judaism are just layers on top of a deeper reason. The reading, study, and discussions I have had have convinced me that offering Judaism and welcoming sincere converts is embedded in the covenant of the Jewish people with God. That is, I believe the Jewish people have a divine obligation to offer those who are interested the opportunity to learn about Judaism. I provide a full explanation of these views in my book *The Theory and Practice of Welcoming Converts to Judaism: Jewish Universalism* (Lewiston, ME: Edwin Mellen Press, 1992), most of which is available on my web site. Let it suffice here to say that these views have been strengthened over the years as I have expanded my efforts.

I recently founded the Conversion to Judaism Resource Center to provide information to Gentiles who are interested in learning about Judaism. This effort, supplementing others, provides fresh daily evidence that Judaism is a vital gateway to meaning for many people, that it is a vibrant and exciting spiritual path, and that, finally, it is a sure path to God, and therefore to understanding the natural world, people, and ourselves. Hearing converts tell me their stories and their struggles makes me wish that I had heard these tales when I was younger and uncertain about the value of Judaism. I invite born Jews with such perceptions to study with converts and, in so doing, rediscover Judaism.

Let me also include a word about language. I remain in the linguistic bind that I have discussed in earlier works. There are some converts who, with valid Talmudic justification, believe that their status is that of someone fully Jewish, and so designations such as "convert" or "proselyte" or "Jew by Choice" are demeaning, inaccurate, and serve to unfairly separate one group of Jews from another. This is compounded by the dictum to Jews that when a conversion has taken place, the person who has converted is fully Jewish and should not be reminded of a prior status as a Gentile. In addition, some linguistic options such as "Choosing Jew" or "New Jew" lack linguistic felicity.

Therefore, using the language that is necessary to write this book is ethically troubling. I do so because I believe it is important to describe the historic phenomenon of large numbers of converts joining the Jewish people. In addition, I have chosen to use the word "convert" to describe those who become Jewish. This is not necessarily a precise term; indeed, it bothers some who have chosen Judaism. Lacking correct language, I have tried to use words that are clear and understandable. However, I want to add that the language I use is not meant to be demeaning, and its use is predicated on the belief that it should not be used to describe anyone who finds it offensive.

So, then, let us turn to the questions.

I
BECOMING JEWISH

1
Who Converts to Judaism?

Q. What is conversion to Judaism?

Epstein. To convert is to change from one identity to another. A conversion to Judaism, however, does not mean that the previous identity was a religious one. Many secular people, born nominally in another religion or having no religion, choose Judaism. Choosing a Jewish identity means taking on a particular set of views and practices, although there is no set, required formula for those views and the practices vary widely among groups of Jews. Still, a conversion means that, within the broad spectrum of accepted Jewish identity, a person chooses to become identified with the history and fate of the Jewish people.

For many converts, conversion means accepting the beliefs and rituals of Judaism as a religion. Core beliefs, such as that of one God, and core practices, such as observing Jewish holy days, are studied and absorbed. This, of course, is a central part of conversion. Learning Jewish beliefs and practices is a principal path to conversion.

However, conversion to Judaism means more than accepting Judaism as a world view. Converting also means joining a people, which involves learning its history, adopting the sensibility of belonging to that people, and learning its particular customs, food tastes, humor, and consciousness. Most of all, conversion means fully identifying with a people, feeling part of it and obliged to it.

This dual notion of conversion—religious and cultural—makes conversion to Judaism both exciting and challenging.

Q. Can people convert to Judaism?

Epstein. All the major branches of Judaism in the United States— Orthodox, Conservative, Reform, and Reconstructionist—recognize the legal validity of conversion to Judaism. These branches differ, sometimes fiercely, about who can conduct conversions, the appropriate motivations for a conversion candidate, the processes of conversion, and so on, but, at least within their own groupings, all recognize the general validity of conversion.

This should not be surprising, since Judaism was founded by Abraham and Sarah, neither of whom were born Jewish. Throughout Jewish history, converts have made major contributions. The Talmud describes how conversions can take place. The authoritative codes of Jewish law, such as the *Shulchan Aruch*, include information about conversion. While in biblical times certain peoples were forbidden to become Jewish, it is now impossible to identify such groups. Therefore, in principle, any Gentile who sincerely accepts Judaism can become Jewish.

Let me tell you some real stories about people who converted to Judaism.

There are about 200,000 people in the United States who have chosen to become Jewish. They join untold numbers of people in Jewish history who have joined the Jewish people, including the most famous one, Ruth. I researched conversion and interviewed hundreds of converts for my book *Conversion to Judaism: A Guidebook* (Northvale, NJ: Jason Aronson Inc., 1994). In their own way, all these people have fascinating stories to tell.

Some of those who have become Jewish are well-known, such as movie stars like Marilyn Monroe, Elizabeth Taylor, and Sammy

Davis, Jr. One famous story about Sammy Davis involves his filming *Porgy and Bess*.

It was not long after his conversion, and he refused to work on Yom Kippur. The director of the movie got angry and called the legendary producer Samuel Goldwyn. Goldwyn immediately called Sammy and wanted to know if it was true about his refusing to work. Sammy said that, as a Jew, he could not work on the Day of Atonement. There was silence for a moment, with Goldwyn no doubt noting to himself that stopping production would cost $30,000, a large sum, then. Finally, Goldwyn said, "Bless you." Production on the film was stopped for Yom Kippur.

Some people who have chosen Judaism have written about their experience or about conversion. Lena Romanoff, for example, is the author of *Your People, My People: Finding Acceptance and Fulfillment as a Jew by Choice* (Philadephia: Jewish Publication Society, 1990). Ms. Romanoff is also a widely known lecturer and counselor who has started several support groups, including her newest one for children of interfaith and conversionary couples. John David Scalamonti was a former priest who, after questioning his faith, eventually fell in love with a Jewish woman. She and her patient family explained Jewish customs to him, and he eventually embraced Judaism. Scalamonti frequently lectures on the great changes in his life and has written about it in his book *Ordained to Be a Jew* (Hoboken, NJ: KTAV, 1992). Catherine Hall Myrowitz has written *Finding a Home for the Soul: Interviews with Converts to Judaism* (Northvale, NJ: Jason Aronson, 1995), in which she presents a wide variety of fascinating stories about people who have embraced Judaism. The well-known black writer Julius Lester wrote of his conversion experiences in his book *Lovesong*. Lydia Kukoff has written a guidebook for converts, *Choosing Judaism*.

Other converts have made important contributions to their congregations or to Jewish life. Ben Asher, for instance, helped organize and ran a now-defunct Rabbinical Assembly 800 number for those interested in learning about the Conservative movement's conversion and outreach programs. Dru Greenwood heads the UAHC-CCAR Commission on Reform Jewish Outreach, which provides information about the movement's conversion and outreach programming.

The Holocaust had a profound effect on many who have converted. Dr. Gilya Gerda Schmidt became Jewish as a response to what she saw as the "crimes committed by my parents' and grandparents' generations." She wanted to replace some of the Jews who had been killed. Then there is the strange case of Reuel Abraham. (An expanded version of this story is told in the section on famous converts.)

Abraham was born a German citizen, with the name Karl Heinz Schneider. At 18, he joined the Nazi air force. One day he saw Nazi storm troopers killing a group of Jews, and he was especially impressed as he saw a rabbi clutching a Torah tightly as he died. Schneider, thoroughly shocked, suddenly realized the horrors of Nazism. He began to disobey orders, dropping bombs into lakes, or fixing them so they wouldn't explode. After the war, he worked in Germany for 20 years as a penance, giving two-thirds of his salary to groups that helped Jewish orphans who had survived the concentration camps. He also began to attend Jewish services. After the 20 years, he sold all he owned and bought a farm in Israel. He then went to the rabbinical authorities in Haifa and asked to be converted. Astonished at his story, the rabbis investigated. When they learned that what he had told them was true, he was allowed to study and ultimately became Jewish and a citizen of Israel.

Not all those who wished to convert had it easy. In the nineteenth century, a man named Warder Cresson was put on trial by his family for insanity after he announced that he wished to convert. Cresson had received an appointment as the first American consul to Jerusalem, and indeed had come to the land of Israel to help missionaries. Once he got there, however, he was overwhelmed at seeing Jews back in their ancient homeland. He converted and returned to his family in Philadelphia. Shocked at his religious passage, they had him declared insane. In a nationally covered trial held in May, 1851, Cresson was declared legally sane. After the trial, Cresson and his wife divorced, and he returned to the land of Israel and married a Sephardic Jewish woman. He worked tirelessly to help the Jews there. All Jewish-owned businesses in Jerusalem were closed on the day he died.

Once in a while the appearance of difficulty in converting can be deceiving. A rabbi told me this story about one of the members of his congregation: A young woman went to her parents, telling them of her desire to become Jewish and marry a Jewish man. The parents were mildly upset, but agreed. They warned her, however, not to tell her grandmother, who was very religious and would not accept her conversion. The young woman loved her grandmother and wanted to be honest with her. She told her grandmother the truth. After hearing the news, the grandmother leaped out of her chair and went into the bedroom. Loud crying could be heard through the door. Upset, the young woman gently knocked at the door, went inside, and expressed her love for her grandmother. The grandmother drew her close. "You don't understand," she sobbed. "I was born a Jew. I have hidden this fact almost my whole life, ever since I married your grandfather. I never told your parents. Nothing could make me happier than you becoming Jewish."

Despite hardships, small and large, thousands of people are drawn to Judaism. Their stories are woven into the fabric of Judaism's majestic history.

Q. How many people have converted to Judaism in the United States?

Epstein. It is difficult to provide exact figures for many reasons. In 1990, the Council of Jewish Federations conducted a National Jewish Population Survey. In that study, 185,000 people in the United States were called "Jews by Choice." This group included those who had formally converted to Judaism and those who considered themselves Jewish but had not gone through a formal religious conversion. This latter group is not considered Jewish by the Jewish community. There is no such activity as a self-conversion, and so this group cannot be truly considered converts.

The survey may have undercounted converts, though, because the way in which a Jewish survey is conducted relies on people having Jewish ethnic names. Thus a convert to Judaism with a "Gentile" name would not have even been called to take part in the survey and so would not be counted.

It is also difficult to judge the number of converts using only anecdotal material. I know that more than 2,000 people a month visit my web site, but some of them will take years to convert, and some are just exploring and will not convert. I also hear from rabbis who are conducting conversion classes. The anecdotal evidence, to me, suggests a higher number than the 5,000 normally given. I think it is fair to estimate that somewhere between 5,000 and 10,000 persons convert to Judaism each year. I would suggest that the number has been growing in the 1990s after dropping in the 1980s.

Q. Who can convert to Judaism?

Epstein. Any sincere person can choose to become Jewish. However, no one can be considered Jewish who also accepts the views of another religion. Thus, for example, someone who believes that Jesus is the messiah embraces a Christian view and therefore would not be accepted as a convert to Judaism. While Judaism is enormously flexible in its understanding of God and permissive in its willingness to allow spiritual speculation, Judaism does have defined limits.

Of course, no conversion candidate would be accepted who believes in ideas antithetical to Jewish existence. No one who supports anti-Semitism or denies Israel's right to exist, for example, would be acceptable to rabbis.

Within these limits, all people are acceptable as conversion candidates. Of course, converts must also be willing to study and adapt to Jewish life. That is, if you do not have theological beliefs contradictory to Judaism, and are willing to identify with the Jewish people, you can begin the study of Judaism.

Q. My ancestors were Jewish. Do I have to convert?

Epstein. According to traditional Jewish law, a person is Jewish if that person's mother is Jewish or if the person formally converts. Therefore, if your mother was Jewish (that is, if her mother was Jewish or if she converted), then you are Jewish and do not need to convert formally.

Since 1983, the Reform movement has accepted the principle of patrilineality, by which a person is considered Jewish both if the person's mother is Jewish or if the person's father is Jewish and the person performs public acts of identification with the Jewish community. The Reconstructionist movement also supports this view, although the Conservative and Orthodox movements oppose it.

If you are uncertain about your legal status, consult a rabbi. You may wish to rejoin the Jewish people in a formal way by undergoing conversion. It is really a reunion rather than a conversion, but the processes are the same.

There are also groups of people about whom the legal status is uncertain. These people, the *anusim*, were once called Marranos, which is a derogatory term used against them and therefore inappropriate. These are the descendants of Jews forcibly converted in Spain and Portugal at the end of the fifteenth century and beginning of the sixteenth. These forced converts went to Africa, Latin America, and elsewhere. Their status as Jews is still being debated within the Jewish community. If you belong to this group, you may want to convert to erase any doubts, although it remains possible that the *anusim* will be declared fully Jewish by religious authorities.

Q. Can a Gentile couple convert?

Epstein. If both partners of a Gentile couple sincerely wish to convert to Judaism, then they can both embark on a study. In some ways, this is an easier conversion because the motivations are clearly sincere, the study can be done together, and partners can grow closer as they embark on this spiritual journey. On the other hand, a Gentile couple may have a very weak or nonexistent Jewish support system if there is no extended Jewish family to provide information or emotional support. It is therefore especially important for a Gentile couple in which both partners want to convert to speak with a rabbi and consciously develop a support system in a synagogue, Jewish Community Center, among Jewish friends, and so on. This support system will be vitally needed as the conversion progresses.

Q. I'm a Gentile romantically involved with someone Jewish. What advantages and disadvantages are there to my converting?

Epstein. There are several advantages, but whatever the advantages, they aren't the reasons to become Jewish. Converting to Judaism involves a serious desire to embrace the faith and the people. It is a simple fact of American life that you do not have to become Jewish, so the reasons to do so must be persuasive. The major reasons have to do with Judaism's great beauty as a religion and way of life. The real "advantage" is that you will have an opportunity to learn about a great spiritual tradition and, if it is right for you, learn how to walk in its path.

Having said that, there are, of course, many practical advantages to conversion. The ones most cited to me when I talk to converts are that the home is religiously united. This is very crucial, for a home with one faith removes a barrier that can emerge later. There are crucial life moments, such as a birth or a death in the family, and holidays, such as Christmas, when the differences can emerge and damage a family. Rabbi Rachel Cowan and Paul Cowan, of blessed memory, called these moments "time bombs" in their book *Mixed Blessings* (New York: Doubleday, 1987). Every marriage has plenty of time bombs waiting to go off. Insofar as these can be defused or removed, the marriage will inevitably be stronger. In that sense, a united faith will reduce marital stress.

Another family advantage, of course, is that children can be brought up in a single faith with no sense that they are having to choose faiths (or, more horribly for them, choose a parent to emulate spiritually). Some interfaith couples decide to raise the children in two faiths, or some children in one and other children in the other, or with no faith, or in some "neutral" faith such as Unitarianism. While individual families are different, the research of Lena Romanoff, author of *Your People, My People* (Philadelphia: Jewish Publication Society, 1990), is impressive. Ms. Romanoff works with, among others, the children of interfaith couples. As I interpret her conclusions, she feels that such couples may be perfectly happy, but their children are not. This bears out my own more anecdotal conclusions. Children may or may not like the faith of their parents, but a single faith is better than none or both. The advantage of choosing Judaism is that such a single faith emerges in the home.

The disadvantages used to be more obvious: a possible encounter with anti-Semitism. Overt, organized anti-Semitism seems to be on the decline and, while anti-Jewish activities persist, they are not as serious or life-threatening as they once were. The disadvantages of conversion are personal ones—a possible sense of having abandoned a birth faith, a sense of strangeness among family and friends, belonging to a minority group in a majority Christian culture. In fact, even these disadvantages are overstated because Jews have integrated so fully and so well into American culture.

On balance, even if the conversion were simply investigated on the basis of family harmony, the advantages would far outweigh the disadvantages. If, as I suggest, the true reasons for conversion—discovering the force and beauty of Jewishness, learning to live a Jewish way of life, and so on—are stronger than the practical, then, from my obviously biased view, the advantages are profoundly greater than any possible disadvantages.

Q. I'm African-American. Can I convert to Judaism?

Epstein. Of course. There are many African-American Jews. One famous convert is Julius Lester, author of the wonderful memoir

Lovesong (New York: Holt, 1988). There are many others. However, the fact that, in principle, an African-American convert to Judaism is no different than any other convert does not mean that there are not special problems in reality. Because of tensions between the African-American and Jewish communities, some African-American converts feel torn between two cultures. Some feel that born Jews are reluctant to accept a non-white convert as genuinely Jewish. On the other hand, there are Jews, such as those associated with the organization KULANU (1211 Ballard Street, Silver Spring, MD 20910; Tel: 301-681-5679), who help lost Jewish communities, including many in Africa, Asia, and Latin America. KULANU deals with many non-white Jews and people who believe they have Jewish ancestors. There are also Jewish communities in the United States where non-white members are commonplace: I remember visiting a synagogue in Hawaii; a black man was handing out the prayer books and there were Asians in the congregation.

Q. I'm Hispanic. Can I convert?

Epstein. The same principles apply as in the question above. There is an increasing population in the United States from Spanish-speaking countries and, no doubt, the interest of some in Judaism will increase. There may also be Jewish ancestors in your family, which you should investigate.

Q. I'm gay. Can I convert?

Epstein. The attitudes among Jews and Jewish groups toward homosexuality vary greatly. The Orthodox, in general, find homosexuality in violation of Jewish law and so remain opposed to homosexual practices. Reform and Reconstructionist Judaism are much more open to homosexuality. Conservative Judaism is more ambivalent. There are also synagogues specifically aimed at gays and lesbians. As in society, attitudes are in flux in the Jewish community. It is important to discuss your feelings openly with a rabbi, to assess where you would be comfortable in terms of a synagogue and movement. When I wrote a previous book, *Conversion to Judaism: A Guidebook* (Northvale, NJ: Jason Aronson, 1994), I heard from about ten gay men who told me of their love of Judaism. Most had Jewish partners, and all seem thrilled with Judaism's intellectual openness and tolerance. There is an emerging literature on the subject of homosexuality in Jewish life, and this should be read with care.

Q. I'm single. Can I convert?

Epstein. Yes, but as with some of the groups above, single people can find some difficulty in feeling attached to the community because of a lack of a family support system. Many Jewish rituals emphasize family life, but single people find those rituals useful and moving. It is particularly crucial to develop contacts within synagogues and Jewish groups. After the conversion, you can join a Jewish singles group if you want to do so.

Q. I'm a Gentile and married to another Gentile. Can I convert?

Epstein. In this case, it is assumed that your Gentile partner does not wish to convert. Many rabbis, especially traditional rabbis, are reluctant to convert people with Gentile partners who are not converting. The reason for this is that once a conversion occurs, there is immediately an intermarriage. Other rabbis are more open, willing to help Gentiles married to other Gentiles. Think through the difficulties you will face in what will be an intermarriage. What will you do during Christmas? How will you feel when you have to light Sabbath candles or attend synagogue or celebrate the Jewish holidays alone? "Normal" problems in a marriage might be exacerbated by religious differences. The "time bombs" discussed above can arise unexpectedly. If, after thoughtful consideration, you're sure you want to proceed, speak with a rabbi.

Q. Why can't a *Kohen* (descendant of an ancient Jewish priest) marry a convert according to traditional Judaism?

Epstein. A *Kohen* is, by tradition, a descendant of Moses's brother Aaron, the first High Priest. According to the Bible (Leviticus 21:7), a *Kohen* had to marry a woman who had never been married. Converts constituted another group of women from whom a *Kohen* could not choose a wife. Again, the original reason for this is from the Bible. Ezekiel said that priests, who served in the Temple and taught and thus were symbols of the whole Jewish people, had to marry Jewish-born women, literally the "seed of the House of Israel." One change by the rabbis in the Talmudic era was that if a priest married the daughter of a convert, the marriage—if it had already taken place—did not have to be dissolved.

Since Reform Judaism does not follow *halachah*, Jewish law, the rules of a *Kohen* do not apply within the Reform movement. Conservative Judaism, which is halachic, has a range of views on what the *halachah* allows. A *Kohen* who wishes to marry a convert and is affiliated with a Conservative synagogue needs to discuss this issue as early as possible with a rabbi.

Q. Can an infant or young child convert?

Epstein. Parents may want to consider converting their infants or children to Judaism for a variety of reasons. Some Jewish parents are intermarried, and the Gentile spouse does not plan to become Jewish, but both parents agree that the single religion of Judaism will be in the child's best interest. Perhaps either a Gentile parent in an intermarriage or a couple made up of two Gentile parents decide to convert to Judaism, but their children were born before the conversion. Perhaps a Jewish couple adopts a Gentile child. In all these cases, conversion to Judaism can be seen as a desirable option for the infants and minor children. A minor child in Jewish law means the child is under age 12 for a female and under age 13 for a male.

In the case of intermarriage, the child of a Jewish woman and her Gentile male spouse is universally recognized as Jewish, and so the conversion of the infant or child is unnecessary. A more delicate and difficult situation arises when the infant or child is born to a Jewish father and Gentile mother. The Orthodox and Conservative movements do not recognize such a child as legally Jewish; in such cases, Orthodox and Conservative parents need to have their child legally converted to Judaism. Under the Reform movement's patrilineality principle, the child of a Jewish father and Gentile mother is presumed Jewish if the child accepts a Jewish identity through public religious acts. The children, then, are legally Jewish. However, some of these Reform parents may voluntarily choose to have their children converted for various reasons, such as wider acceptance of their children's Jewishness by the non-Reform Jewish community.

Jewish parents in all movements need to convert adopted Gentile minors for the minors to be considered Jewish. The adoption itself, or even the raising of the child as Jewish, does not make the child Jewish.

The conversion of an infant or child has Jewish legal sanction. According to the Talmud (Ketubot 11a), it is permissible for a religious court (a *Bet Din*) to convert a gentile infant. The basis in Jewish law is that it is a privilege to be Jewish (Shulchan Aruch, Yoreh Deah, 268:7). Therefore, a minor can be converted even though not mature enough to understand the act because making the minor Jewish is performing a favor for that infant or child. Jewish law also allows those people converted as an infant or child to renounce the conversion when they reach maturity. After girls reach 12 or boys 13, converted infants and children can legally reject the conversion and go back to their previous religion. If they accept Judaism or are silent, they are deemed to be considered adult converts.

One potential problem for parents seeking to convert minors is that not all movements accept conversions performed by rabbis in other movements. Thus, Orthodox rabbis, for example, do not, in general, accept conversions performed by non-Orthodox rabbis. Conservative rabbis, in general, accept all Orthodox conversions and all Reform conversions, if the Reform conversions conform to the Conservative legal requirements discussed in this section. Reform rabbis, in general, recognize all conversions performed by Orthodox and Conservative rabbis. Because of this confusing situation, parents ought to discuss their choice with their rabbi.

The conversion of a female infant or child according to Conservative and Orthodox practices only requires *tevilah* (immersion in a ritual bath called a *mikvah*).

A male child also requires immersion in the *mikvah*. Prior to the immersion, the male must have a *brit milah* (a legal circumcision ceremony performed by a *mohel*, the person trained to perform ritual circumcisions). If possible, this should be done on the eighth day after the birth of the boy. If a circumcision has already been performed, a drop of blood needs to be drawn in a ceremony called *hatafat dam brit*. A Hebrew name can then be given to the child, although some wait to give the name until after the *tevilah* ceremony. There is usually a wait of a couple of weeks between the circumcision and the immersion.

A *Bet Din*, usually consisting of three rabbis, is convened for the immersion. Parents can enter the *mikvah*. If the children are old enough, they recite the needed prayers; if not, a rabbi does so for them. After the *tevilah* ceremony is completed, and a name chosen if one has not already been selected, the child is declared by the Bet Din to be Jewish.

Reform requirements for the conversion of infants and children vary. Some rabbis may simply have a naming ceremony, while others will include some or all of the same requirements used by the Orthodox and Conservative rabbis.

For detailed explanation of all of these ceremonies, it is crucial to consult a rabbi.

The conversion of infants and children is, of course, a moment of joy for parents, but it is also such a moment for the entire Jewish community. New children add precious lives to the community and bring with them that most valuable idea of hope for the future.

Q. Why does an adopted infant whose parents aren't known go through conversion?

Epstein. It is a benefit for the adopted child whose parents aren't known to be a Gentile so that there is no concern for the family connections of the infant, and thus the possible illegal unions that could occur. The presumption of Gentile status makes conversion a requirement.

Q. Is the baby of a convert who was pregnant at the time she converted to Judaism also considered Jewish?

Epstein. When a woman converts, the conversion is only for her, and thus any children she has already had, of whatever age, must undergo a separate conversion as described above. Any child born after a conversion ceremony is born a Jewish infant. Thus the pregnant convert who completes her conversion prior to the birth does not have to have a separate conversion ceremony for the newborn.

Q. I practice Judaism and feel Jewish. Do I have to convert in a formal way?

Epstein. It's wonderful that you feel so attached to Jewish life and Jewish practices. You are like a visitor to a country who likes the people and the customs and wants to be a citizen. In order to do so, you need to undergo the formal requirements of such citizenship. Similarly, in Judaism, in order to be really Jewish, you must go through a formal conversion ceremony. The fact that you already practice should help accelerate the process. It is important to speak to a rabbi and officially join the people to whom you already feel attached.

2
Reasons for Conversion

Q. Why do people convert to Judaism?

Epstein. People decide to become Jewish for a very wide variety of reasons. Some come to Judaism after a long spiritual search. Many people who eventually convert had their interest sparked because of a romantic relationship with someone Jewish. Among the reasons most given by people who do convert are:

1. Judaism has sensible religious beliefs.
2. Becoming Jewish allows converts to share the faith of their partners.
3. Becoming Jewish unites the family through religion.
4. Becoming Jewish will make it easier for children by giving them a clear religious identity.

Think about your own reasons. Remember, conversion must be your own free choice, not done because of pressure, but out of a genuine desire to embrace Judaism.

Learn as much as you can about Judaism. Read as much as you can about Judaism. Go to lectures, take introductory courses on Judaism offered by many colleges, Jewish Community Centers,

Jewish congregations, and other adult education programs, and talk to some Jewish friends. Judaism has an important ethnic component. Becoming a Jew means you are joining a people, not just a religion, and so you need to learn about different aspects of Jewish culture and about Israel.

Also, see if Judaism's basic beliefs and practices make sense to you. Judaism is a faith of good deeds, not forced creeds. There is more concern in Judaism that you act morally than that you have specific beliefs. All Jews share a passion to make the world a better place. It is impossible to summarize Judaism in one brief response, but to get you started, here are some general, widely held Jewish beliefs:

1. Judaism introduced the world to the idea that God is one, not many, and is kind, loving, and personal. In Judaism you pray directly to God and can receive help, guidance, and understanding. You can pray on your own and with a prayer community in a synagogue. Judaism accepts the idea of a covenant, or agreement, between God and the Jewish people.
2. Judaism doesn't accept the idea that people are born evil. Rather, people have free will to choose between right and wrong.
3. Judaism encourages religious freedom of thought. Judaism welcomes probing spiritual questions.
4. Judaism has, for 4,000 years, emphasized a strong sense of family and the value of a close community.

One reason that people are attracted to Judaism is found in their search for spirituality. Let me discuss some of the spiritual reasons why people become Jewish.

It is widely assumed that converts come to Judaism primarily because of a romantic motive, such as to marry a Jewish partner. Rarely, however, does a conversion occur only for such motives. More commonly, conversion ensues after a probing spiritual survey.

I interviewed or received questionnaires from hundreds of converts for my book *Conversion to Judaism: A Guidebook* (1994). A clear pattern emerged of the sorts of experiences felt by converts that might broadly be considered spiritual.

In many cases, people felt that in embracing Judaism they were not so much changing religion as finally identifying their true self. It's as though they had been trapped in a Gentile body by mistake. One neighbor of mine who converted calls herself a "corrected cosmic error." Carol Roth, another convert, says: "I truly believe I was genetically uprooted and born into the wrong family. Somehow in my past I came from Jewish ancestry and the act of conversion was really like going home to my roots."

This feeling of really being Jewish was eventually discovered by these and many other people. The moment of discovery, the beginning of the uplifting journey to Judaism, had come in a variety of ways. What surprised me was how many converts discovered this feeling while reading. As Joanne Stevens put it, "Reading Milton Steinberg's *Basic Judaism* late into the night one evening, I finished the book and said, 'My goodness, I'm a Jew.'" Other converts mentioned books like *Exodus*.

There were a very wide variety of other sources. Some people responded to music at a service. Two people told me that it was the healing nature of Jewish funeral practices that made them want to explore Judaism. Many people mentioned being invited to a Jewishly festive occasion such as a Sabbath meal or a seder. A large number of people found a kinship to someone Jewish. Jean Lund, for example, wrote me about a gentle Jewish man she had known who had been taken prisoner and murdered during World War II. The young man was 18. For 50 years, Ms. Lund has carried his memory as a model of how Judaism can produce virtuous and kind people.

One intriguing group of converts felt a personal connection to those Jews who perished in the Holocaust. This was not a profound sympathy or even empathy, but a deeper sense, that, as one woman put it, she had actually been in the camps, had stood there with her family. One convert told me of her nightmares. She saw Nazi soldiers coming at her. Another mentioned being emotionally overwhelmed at Anne Frank's house in Amsterdam. Some converts articulated a belief that they were replacing Jews either who had died or who had never been born but would have had the Holocaust not taken place.

Of course, many converts felt the guidance of God in their spiritual voyages. Interestingly, though, the overtly religious experiences were ones in which the potential convert was gently, almost invisibly, embraced. The converts I spoke with did not talk of a sudden incursion of God into their lives demanding they become Jewish. Their journeys were slower, more extended, with peak experiences as described above intermingling with longer periods of reflection, uncertainty, confusion, and tremendous excitement in trying to solve the ultimate cosmic mysteries, the ones of meaning and love.

Through all these ways, then, people have come to Judaism. Their spiritual experiences were not limited, though, to their decision to become Jewish. Once they decided to convert, some found additional spiritual experiences.

One such experience that is virtually folkloric by now is that many converts found—only after making the decision to become Jewish—that, in fact, they had Jewish ancestors. This seeming statistical oddity has occurred so often that it merits further study.

Entering the waters of the *mikvah*, or ritual bath, was a deeply spiritual moment for many converts. Such an experience of saying prayers, total immersion, and emerging as a Jew is, of course, an emotionally moving experience. The spiritual element, however, went beyond that. Converts spoke to me of feeling a Jewish soul coming into their bodies in the *mikvah*, replacing the Gentile soul they were cleansing from them. The obvious birth symbolism of the immersion was rendered quite real for many converts. They saw themselves literally as being born in that moment. It is for this reason that I mention to converts who are not required by their rabbi to enter the *mikvah* that they should consider doing so.

As converts finish the process of joining the Jewish people and become fully Jewish, their spiritual experiences fall into the familiar patterns of Jewish life. They have shed one identity and accepted another. Yet in their spiritual journeys the converts have provided for born Jews the crucial insight that born Jews are profoundly fortunate to have inherited the extraordinary religious treasure of Judaism. Seeing others struggle to have a share in that Jewish heritage should make born Jews rediscover the boundless spiritual spheres that Judaism invites its adherents to explore. That, finally, is the special spiritual gift given by converts to the Jewish community.

Q. What are the particular appeals of Judaism?

Epstein. Judaism has several unique aspects. It focuses on a pure monotheism, a single God. It has the notion of a Shabbat, a series of unique holy days, such as Chanukah and Passover. It sees a relationship between the people and God. This relationship forms a covenant, an agreement. Jews feel an obligation to obey God and work with God to repair the world, to make this world better. Thus, becoming a Jew means adopting these practices and this world view.

While practices vary widely within various movements, all the movements have their own ways of marking off key holy moments in Jewish life, such as birth and death, holy days, and all else that marks off Judaism. All the movements, in their own way, see the effort to improve the world ethically as important for the Jewish people.

Of course, the history of the Jewish people itself is unique. Never has such a small people had so vital, so central, an influence on all humanity. Never has a people survived intact for so long under such horrible conditions. Joining the Jewish people means becoming part of this story, entering its exciting spiritual journey.

Jews are rightfully proud of the many contributions Jews have made, the great writers and thinkers, the Nobel Prize winners and others.

3

Thinking about Conversion

Q. I'm uncertain about converting. What should I do?

Epstein. It is common for people to have doubts when they are contemplating such a major step as conversion to Judaism. It is useful to make a checklist of positive reasons to convert and remaining concerns. Is the uncertainty, for example, religious? Perhaps you have trouble giving up a belief in Jesus. Perhaps the uncertainty is not focused, just uncertainty about the future or if the conversion is right for you. As you talk and think through your options with family and friends, you should consider talking about the uncertainty with a rabbi or counselor. It is crucial to understand that you can begin a study of Judaism and go far along the road without committing yourself to a conversion. It is sometimes the case that a person, for example, completes an Introduction to Judaism or conversion class and only then decides that the doubts are too strong to continue. I, personally, think doubt is not the opposite of certainty but a useful part of seeking it. Doubts make you think through conversionary issues, slow down the process to give you time. Clearly, if we waited in life to act with total certainty we would end up doing very little. To paraphrase the nineteenth century writer Samuel Butler, the task of life is to make decisions with too little information.

Q. How do I know if Judaism is right for me?

Epstein. No one can provide a guarantee that a particular way of life is right for you. In a certain way, the answer depends on a personal response after Judaism is lived. The practical suggestion that emerges from this is that those considering conversion should explore Jewish customs and practices within the movement you are considering or in general. You might, for example, celebrate the Sabbath or a holiday, attend a synagogue service or a class or lecture on Judaism, read Jewish books, see Jewish videos, listen to Jewish music, visit a Jewish site, try Jewish foods, and so on. Only really by leading the life can you see if it is right for you, and you can, to some extent at least, rehearse a Jewish life before you actually convert. I suggest people contemplating conversion take an Introduction to Judaism or conversion class. As indicated in the previous answer, attending the class doesn't require you to convert, but everyone I have been in contact with tells me they enjoyed the class even if only because it made them think about their spiritual lives and views. Even people who don't ultimately convert find the process a true search for self and therefore extremely gratifying.

Q. I'm scared, confused, and feel overwhelmed. Are these common feelings?

Epstein. I've heard these feelings expressed by a large number of people who are converting. They are very common and very understandable. Let me quote a brief section from my book *Conversion to Judaism: A Guidebook* (1994), in which I start with a real anecdote about just such a feeling.

> Bob had been raised as an Italian Catholic but had drifted away. It was only while studying to become Jewish that he thought about the heritage of his birth. He felt guilt at leaving it and a loss of his own background. This feeling precipitated a series of conflicts about converting in the first place. Finally, Bob realized that his Jewish

identity was the one that represented how he truly felt. A counselor led Bob through a "mourning process," by which he gradually came to terms with his sense of loss through a self-examination of who he was, what he wanted out of life, why he was converting. As in all stages, Bob's support group and a model—someone whose conversion has been successful—were also of great help.

Bob's loss was analogous to a death, the death of part of one's past. That is why Judaism sees conversion as a sort of rebirth, a chance to begin life again. Seen as a new opportunity and fresh start, his conversion gave hope to Bob.

I also wrote about the frequently reported sense of being overwhelmed. Such a feeling can be both emotional and intellectual.

Emotionally, the change of identity is so unsettling that it is common to feel that the entire experience is beyond one's ability to handle. Intellectually, Judaism is filled with history and customs, some or much of which is foreign and difficult for those coming to it for the first time. Many born Jews do not know a lot about Judaism, but conversion candidates often express concern that they do not really know enough to be Jewish.

Another feeling that is frequently expressed is one of marginality, of feeling like an outsider, a feeling of continuing uncertainty about one's genuine religious identity. I wrote:

This often happens soon after the conversion process has been completed and is sensed as not really feeling Jewish, or feeling neither Jewish nor Christian. In the former case, the person may legally be Jewish, but internally there is a sense that the person's root reactions, instincts, and sensibilities—one's central identity—are not yet Jewish. This feeling of belonging frequently just takes time. It comes with performing Jewish tasks, raising Jewish children, thinking Jewishly. One woman told me she knew she was really Jewish when she found herself rushing to the television to hear a news report about Israel, something she never would have done prior to her conversion.

"The usual antidote suggested for these feelings is joining Jewish life." I still feel like this. The feelings are common. They are signals the brain is sending, they need to be listened to, and they deserve a response. Don't ignore them. On the other hand, don't let them paralyze you. Discuss the feelings with friends, family, a rabbi, or a professional counselor.

Q. I don't like the word "convert." Do I have to use it?

Epstein. As I wrote in the Introduction to this book, there is no truly correct and useful language with which to talk about joining the Jewish people. No single term in English is good. *Proselyte* was a Greek neologism to translate the Hebrew word *ger*, which really means a stranger. People often don't understand the term *proselyte*. I described the problems with "convert" or "Jew by Choice" or other terms. You certainly do not have to use any term you find distasteful, but you should forgive well-meaning people who do use the terminology. Perhaps as more and more people become Jewish, a useful group of words will emerge. Until then, we must all struggle not to offend but to enlighten with the confusing language we do have.

Q. I've decided to convert to Judaism. How do I tell my parents, family, and friends?

Epstein. There is no right answer to the question of when to tell people about your decision to convert to Judaism. In this response, I am going to discuss telling your parents about the conversion, although these general ideas can be applied to telling others as well.

People vary greatly in their approach to telling a parent. Some write a letter. Others talk over dinner. Some drop hints, such as giving books on Judaism, to get their parents used to the idea of conversion. Some never tell a parent.

You should decide, in consultation with a partner, a rabbi, a trusted friend, or a counselor about the best approach for you. I have asked various people with a lot of experience about this issue.

This response is a summary of their views. Do not, however, take these suggestions as the ones you should necessarily follow. You need, most of all, to trust your own judgment. Only you know the situation best. Here, then, are the suggestions:

1. Think through your feelings. Practice talking them out. Consider rehearsing before telling your parents.
2. Most experts think telling parents in person and to both parents at the same time is best. Obviously, this is the very moment that many people find the most difficult. If this is not possible, consider alternatives.
3. Telling your parents as soon as possible is best. The danger in delay, such as by only dropping hints at first, is that your parents will hear about the conversion from others or unintentionally provide awkward moments at family gatherings. Ideally, telling parents should be done prior to a wedding to allow all parents to participate in the planning of the wedding. Such participation reenforces the idea that parents are not being abandoned.
4. There is no special time to tell. Of course, such an announcement shouldn't be made during days of obvious religious significance, such as Easter or Christmas, or even those of obvious personal significance such as a birthday or anniversary.
5. There is a difference of opinion among those with whom I spoke about whether to bring a Jewish partner to the discussion. Most people said it was better to speak to parents alone. Others needed the support and help their partners gave during this potentially difficult time.
6. In telling your parents about your conversion, discuss what you find attractive about Judaism, how it met a particular need, how it helped a relationship, how you feel closer to, not further from, your parents, in part because of Judaism's emphasis on family. Make it clear that it was your choice to convert and the conversion was not due to emotional pressure from your partner or partner's family. This statement of your reasons needs to be accompanied by reassuring your

family of your continuing love, of the obvious fact that you will always be their child and be part of the family. Some parents feel they are being rejected, so it is crucial to tell them that is not the case.

7. Be prepared for a range of reactions from support to shock to total disapproval. In general, remain calm, show an understanding of any resistance to the idea of converting, and stick to your views. Be polite, but firm.

8. Follow up a visit with a letter or phone call.

The vast majority of converts with whom I have spoken report that they received support from their parents, or some initial resistance and then support. There were cases, however, of continuing resistance.

If your parents do reject your religious conversion, remember that parents may in time change. In the meanwhile, seek support from your partner and from within the Jewish community while constantly seeking continued communication with your parents.

Perhaps most of all, try to maintain a sense of humor and a clear display of love.

4

Asking Someone
to Consider Conversion

Q. How do I ask someone to consider becoming Jewish?

Epstein. You may know someone who might be interested in learning about Judaism. Perhaps it is a non-Jewish spouse, or someone married to your child, or another relative of yours.

You would like to discuss conversion to Judaism with that person. You may have many reasons for this. Perhaps you regard Judaism as so wonderful you want a loved one to share it. Maybe, you're just proud of being Jewish. Maybe, you think a family should share a similar religion. Perhaps you think the children in such a relationship will benefit from a Jewish heritage.

There are some general guidelines for you to follow in discussing becoming Jewish.

- The most important aspect of discussing conversion is not to be afraid or reluctant to discuss the subject. Most non-Jews are never even asked if they would consider learning about Judaism. Many would do so if they were simply asked to explore the subject.

- Remember that conversion is a long process, and not a single action. Becoming Jewish can be exciting and fun, but it is a decision that will require long-term support. Conversion, after all, means changing religion and joining a new people.
- Because a welcoming attitude is the most important contribution you can make, remember not to use any emotional pressure. Conversion is a personal decision, to be carefully considered. Instead of pressure, focus on showing love and humor, two vital Jewish qualities of special importance when dealing with conversion.

Now, it's on to the specifics of how to discuss the subject of conversion. There are several steps for you to take.

1. Consider why you think being Jewish is important, and, in particular, why being affiliated with a particular movement in Judaism matters to you if this is appropriate to your situation. Different people will have very different answers to these questions. Some people like the beauty of Jewish rituals. Others admire and identify with the brave history of the Jewish people. Still others believe the Jewish faith helps them understand and deal with life. Explore your own reasons.
2. Consider why you wish the person you care about to become Jewish. How will becoming Jewish help that person? What positive contributions to the person's life, marriage, and family relationships will be made by becoming Jewish? The answers to these, of course, will depend on the person.
3. Decide on the best time to approach the subject of conversion. In general, it is important to raise the subject as early as possible in a serious relationship. Important moments in a family's history provide good times to discuss conversion. Such moments include when the non-Jewish person is to be engaged or married to someone Jewish, or is married and a child is expected. Bad times include non-Jewish religious holidays.

4. There isn't a single correct way to ask someone to consider becoming Jewish. One way is to go to a nice restaurant, saying you wish to discuss something you care about, or that you've been thinking about the family. After explaining why being Jewish is important, you might say something like, "Would you consider sharing the Jewish way of life?" The question could be followed by a discussion of the benefits of becoming Jewish for the person. Other possibilities include inviting the person to a seder, or a Bat or Bar Mitzvah, or discussing conversion while talking about plans for having a family. It is also possible to give introductory books about Jewish life or about conversion as a present to the person.

5. Be willing to answer questions, give help when it is requested, and provide constant support. For example, it is important to reassure people that conversion does not mean that they must lose touch with their parents, brothers, and sisters. Nor does it mean that happy memories of childhood need to be forgotten. Also, don't be embarrassed if you are asked questions about Judaism and you do not know the answer. Learning about Judaism together can be fun and a way to strengthen a relationship.

6. If the person expresses an interest in learning, there are several important steps to take. The best first step is to have a talk with a friendly rabbi. Perhaps a family member knows such a rabbi. Some additional early activities include attending a Sabbath dinner and service; going to a Jewish ceremony, such as a wedding; taking part in a Jewish holiday, such as by lighting Chanukah candles; taking an Introduction to Judaism class; visiting Jewish sites; reading about Judaism; watching films about Judaism; listening to Jewish music; and others.

Because conversion is a complicated subject, all the questions about it, such as the different movements within Judaism, can't be answered here. Rather, you should discuss them with a rabbi. For example, the person who is considering conversion will want to know details about its Jewish requirements. This is the kind of question that should be discussed in detail with your rabbi. In general, depending on the movement in which you are interested in joining, these requirements may include sponsorship by a rabbi, a period of study in which Jewish history and practices and other material are learned, a circumcision for a male or a symbolic one done by drawing a drop of blood if one has already been performed, an appearance before a religious court called a *Bet Din*, immersion in water, and a final ceremony including getting a Hebrew name. It is also important to read books about conversion, if possible talk to people who have become Jewish, and discuss the subject with family.

There are about 200,000 people in the United States who have chosen to become Jewish. They did so because they found Judaism to be a wonderful way of life and because they found Jewish people, like you, who welcomed them.

Q. How can I ask my romantic partner to convert? I wouldn't convert to another religion.

Epstein. First of all, your romantic partner has every right to say "No, thanks" as you would if you were asked. Secondly, your partner may not feel as strongly about retaining religious ties as you do. Many born Jews, even those who do not follow traditional religious practices, have a very strong ethnic or cultural tie to Judaism. Their concept of conversion is leaving one people to join another, a step they would not do. However, many Gentiles do not have such an identity, and their religious identity may be unformed. Indeed, many converts have told me they loved the process of conversion because, often for the first time in their lives, they got to think through their religious beliefs. Finally, consider the motives for asking. If what you want is a stronger family life, a sense of clear identity for your children, a shared set of values with your spouse, then conversion is a reasonable option for your partner to consider.

One factor that is important here is simply demographic. There are, perhaps, about 6 million American Jews, comprising about 2 percent of the American population. Thus, each Jew becomes precious not just as a human being (as are all human beings) but as a member of a minuscule group. Any step that can be taken to help the Jewish community is important. The conversion to Judaism of non-Jewish spouses will help the Jewish community and simultaneously will not harm a Gentile community.

I once was told of a priest who was asked to counsel an interfaith couple. The born-Catholic woman and the Jewish man were engaged. The woman had attended church and wanted the priest's advice since the couple had read the literature and concluded that a single-religion family was stronger for any children. The priest agreed with the conclusion and advised the couple to raise the children as Jewish because the Jewish community faced a loss of numbers that, because of its size, endangered its continuity. The surprised couple agreed with this conclusion.

As long as a request is made without emotional or other kind of pressure, it is fair to ask someone to consider Judaism. You might add as part of your question that you yourself wouldn't convert and that you therefore feel awkward doing the asking.

Some people request that a rabbi or family member raise the issue, or they purchase a book on conversion to Judaism as a present for their romantic partner.

5

Getting Information and Advice about Conversion and Judaism

Q. How do I begin learning about Judaism?

Epstein. Consider the best way you learn about any new subject. For some, this will mean talking to people. Of course, the best person to talk with is a rabbi.

I've noticed that since I began the Conversion to Judaism Home Page <http://www.convert.org>, many people have used the site not only to get basic information but to ask me questions anonymously. One of the best parts of that site are the rabbis who answer questions posed to them. There is a section on America Online where this is also done. That is a great way to ask questions to authorities without having even to identify yourself!

I'm a book person, so when I approach a new subject I always read about it. Some reading suggestions are included in the next question.

Some people attend lectures, take classes, visit Jewish sites, and so on.

Whatever your approach, I know from talking with many people who have investigated Judaism that you will enjoy the journey whether or not you ultimately decide to convert.

Q. What books about conversion and Judaism can I read?

Epstein. You can acquire Jewish books in a local synagogue library or at a Jewish bookstore. Many books are available at public libraries. Bookstores can order copies of these books, and they may be requested at libraries through inter-library loans.

Encyclopedias

Roth, C., and Wigoder, G. eds. (1972). *Encyclopaedia Judaica*. 16 vols. Jerusalem: Keter.
Wigoder, G. (1989). *The Encyclopedia of Judaism*. New York: Macmillan.

Introductions to Judaism

Diamant, A., and Cooper, H. (1991). *Living a Jewish Life*. New York: Harper.
Heschel, A. J. (1987). *God in Search of Man*. Northvale, NJ: Jason Aronson.
Jacobs, L. (1984). *The Book of Jewish Belief*. New York: Behrman House.
———. (1987). *The Book of Jewish Practice*. West Orange, NJ: Behrman House.
Prager, D., and Telushkin, J. (1981). *The Nine Questions People Ask about Judaism*. New York: Simon & Schuster.
Siegel, R., Strassfeld, M., and Strassfeld, S. (1973). *The Jewish Catalog*. Philadelphia: Jewish Publication Society.
Steinberg, M. (1987). *Basic Judaism*. Northvale, NJ: Jason Aronson.
Trepp, L. (1980). *The Complete Book of Jewish Observance*. New York: Behrman House/Summit Books.

Sacred Texts

Holtz, B. (1985). *Back to the Sources*. New York: Summit.

Steinsaltz, A. (1992). *The Essential Talmud*. Northvale, NJ: Jason
   Aronson.
Tanakh (1985). Philadelphia: Jewish Publication Society.

Jewish History

Seltzer, R. M. (1980). *Jewish People, Jewish Thought*. New York:
   Macmillan & Collier.

Holocaust

Dawidowicz, L. S. (1975). *The War against the Jews*. New York: Holt,
   Rinehart, and Winston.
Wiesel, E. (1960). *Night*. New York: Hill and Wang.

Israel

Hertzberg, A. (1972). *The Zionist Idea*. New York: Atheneum.
Laqueur, W. (1972). *A History of Zionism*. New York: Holt, Rinehart,
   and Winston.

Jewish Women

Heschel, S. (1983). *On Being a Jewish Feminist*. New York: Schocken.
Plaskow, J. (1991). *Standing Again at Sinai*. San Francisco: Harper.
Schneider, S. W. (1984). *Jewish and Female*. New York: Simon &
   Schuster.

Novels

Antin, M. (1997). *The Promised Land*. New York: Penguin.
Cahan, A. (1993). *The Rise of David Levinsky*. New York: Penguin.
Kellerman, F. (1986). *The Ritual Bath*. New York: Arbor House.
Michener, J. (1965). *The Source*. New York: Random House.
Ozick, C. (1971). *The Pagan Rabbi and Other Stories*. New York:
   Knopf.

Roth, H. (1991). *Call It Sleep*. New York: Farrar, Straus & Giroux.
Singer, I. B. (1957). *Gimpel the Fool*. New York: Noonday Press.
Wouk, H. (1955). *Marjorie Morningstar*. Garden City, NY: Doubleday.

Cookbooks

Bishov, B. K. (1973). *Complete American-Jewish Cookbook*. New York: World.
Leonard, L. (1949). *Jewish Cookery*. New York: Crown.

Books about Conversion to Judaism

Berkowitz, Rabbi A. L., and Moskovitz, P., eds. (1994). *Embracing the Covenant: Converts to Judaism Talk about Why & How*. Woodstock, VT: Jewish Lights Publishing.

Diamant, A. (1997). *Choosing a Jewish Life: A Handbook for People Converting to Judaism and for Their Family and Friends*. New York: Schocken Books.

Epstein, L. J. (1992). *The Theory and Practice of Welcoming Converts to Judaism: Jewish Universalism*. Lewiston, ME: Edwin Mellen Press.

———. (1994). *Conversion to Judaism: A Guidebook*. Northvale, NJ: Jason Aronson.

Fink, N. (1997). *Stranger in the Midst: A Memoir of Spiritual Discovery*. New York: Basic Books.

Forster, B., and Tabachnik, J. (1991). *Jews by Choice: A Study of Converts to Reform and Conservative Judaism*. Hoboken, NJ: KTAV.

Isaacs, Rabbi R. H. (1993). *Becoming Jewish: A Handbook for Conversion*. New York: Rabbinical Assembly.

Kling, S. (1987). *Embracing Judaism*. New York: Rabbinical Assembly.

Kukoff, L. (1981). *Choosing Judaism*. New York: Hippocrene Books.

Lamm, M. (1991). *Becoming a Jew*. Middle Village, NY: Jonathan David.

McClain, E. J. (1995). *Embracing the Stranger: Intermarriage and the Future of the American Jewish Community*. New York: Basic Books.

Myrowitz, C. H. (1995). *Finding a Home for the Soul: Interviews with Converts to Judaism.* Northvale, NJ: Jason Aronson.

Romanoff, L., with Hostein, L. (1990). *Your People, My People: Finding Acceptance and Fulfillment as a Jew by Choice.* Philadelphia: Jewish Publication Society.

Silverstein, Rabbi A. (1995). *It All Begins with a Date: Jewish Concerns about Intermarriage.* Northvale, NJ: Jason Aronson.

————. (1995). *Preserving Jewishness in Your Family: After Intermarriage Has Occurred.* Northvale, NJ: Jason Aronson.

Q. Are there any free pamphlets about conversion?

Epstein. You can get the free pamphlets "Should I Convert to Judaism?" and "How to Discuss Conversion to Judaism" by writing to the Conversion to Judaism Resource Center, 74 Hauppauge Road, Room 53, Commack, NY 11725, (516) 462–5826.

Q. Is there a web site about conversion?

Epstein. The web site that I developed is the Conversion to Judaism Home Page <http://www.convert.org>. The site includes a very wide variety of material about conversion to Judaism. If you have any questions about this site or about conversion to Judaism, you can e-mail me at inform@convert.org and I'll try to respond to your questions.

Q. Is there a discussion group on the Internet about conversion?

Epstein. There are various sites on the internet about conversion in some way or another. For an up-to-date list of sites with conversion materials, check out my web site described above.

Q. What else on the Internet is there for me to learn about Judaism?

Epstein. There are now various guides to Jewish information on the net. Check a local Jewish bookstore. There are links from my web site to much Jewish material. I particularly like the Jewish Communications Network <http://www.jcn18.com> as a source of Jewish news and interesting features. From my site, you can go there and to Judaism 101, which provides basic information about Judaism as well as other places. Explore the net using a Jewish search engine, and you'll discover a wonderful Jewish world on the web.

Q. I like movies. What videos are available for learning about Judaism?

Epstein. Here are just a few of the many motion pictures about Jewish life.

Avalon (Tristar, 1990): a family film about immigrant life in Baltimore, with only limited explicit reference to Jewish values.

Cast a Giant Shadow (Batjac, 1966): the exciting story of Mickey Marcus, an American who helped Israel.

The Chosen (Contemporary, 1981): a warm film of Orthodox Jewish life.

Conspiracy of Hearts (Paramount, 1960): a lovely film about how nuns in a convent hid Jews in wartime Italy.

Diary of Anne Frank (20th Century Fox, 1959): a deeply moving film based on the life of the famous Jewish teenager who hid from the Nazis.

Exodus (United Artists, 1960): a sweeping epic, based on the novel, about Israel's birth.

Fiddler on the Roof (Mirisch, 1971): a musical describing Rus-

sian-Jewish life at the end of the nineteenth century. The
music cannot be resisted.

The Fixer (MGM, 1968): the true story, based on Bernard Mala-
mud's novel, of a Russian Jew in prison for killing a Christian child.

The Frisco Kid (Warner Bros., 1979): a funny movie about a rabbi
from Poland who joins up with an outlaw in the American
West.

Garden of the Finzi-Continis (CCC FilmKunst, 1970): a movie
about the Holocaust in Italy.

Gentleman's Agreement (20th Century Fox, 1947): a famous
movie about anti-Semitism in the 1940s. Gregory Peck
plays a writer who pretends to be Jewish to see how people
will react.

Hester Street (Midwest Films, 1975): a wonderful film about life
on the Lower East Side of New York at the turn of the century.

Judgment at Nuremberg (United Artists, 1961): an outstanding
film about the trials of Nazi war criminals.

The Juggler (Columbia, 1953): the story of a Jewish immigrant,
starring Kirk Douglas, who has difficulty adjusting to Israeli life after the Holocaust.

Lies My Father Told Me (Pentacle VIII, 1975): a warm and telling glimpse of Jewish family life.

Me and the Colonel (Columbia, 1958): a hilarious film starring
Danny Kaye as a Jewish refugee who must join a Polish
aristocratic anti-Semite to escape the Nazis.

Night and Fog (Alain Resnais, 1955): a devastating documentary
about the Holocaust showing horrible scenes of destruction and death.

The Pawnbroker (Landau Co., 1965): a powerful movie about a
Jewish pawnbroker's painful memories of the Holocaust.

School Ties (Paramount, 1992): the story of a student facing anti-
Semitism in a prep school.

Yentl (MGM, 1983): Barbra Streisand's loving rendition of the
work by Isaac Bashevis Singer about a Jewish girl living in
a time when women were not allowed to study holy texts.

Q. Where can I get Jewish music?

Epstein. There are many different ways by which people enter Jewish life. Some people are attracted by the beautiful music of Jewish prayer or culture. There are a very large number of Jewish composers, musicians, and singers, and although not all wrote specifically Jewish songs, a Jewish sensibility underlies a lot of their work. People like Harold Arlen, Irving Berlin, Leonard Bernstein, Bob Dylan, and others have ultimately absorbed a tremendous amount from their Jewish heritage. Many specifically Jewish musicians, like Debbie Friedman, are fascinating performers. For specific works, check a local Jewish bookstore or synagogue shop.

Q. Do I really need to learn Hebrew in order to convert?

Epstein. Many converts (and born Jews) have told me they have a great deal of difficulty learning Hebrew. Perhaps it is American culture, or the fact that the language is being learned as an adult, or a personal learning block. For various reasons, Hebrew is a stumbling block for many.

You may have heard the story of the little girl in synagogue during prayers. She didn't know Hebrew, but she had just learned the Hebrew alphabet. She began reciting it over and over. Her mother looked down at her and asked the little girl what she was doing. The girl looked up and said, "This is all I know, but I figure if I say all the letters, God will put them in the right order."

In Judaism, you are permitted to pray in any language. Hebrew, however, is special, since it is the language of almost all of the Bible and Jewish prayers. The good news is that prayer services (with some holiday exceptions) repeat the same prayers each time that service is given. Therefore, if you learn just a few prayers, you will be able to follow at least part of the service.

Start slowly and keep going. Judaism is often compared to a

ladder. It's less important which rung you are on now than that you are looking up and trying always for that next rung.

There is new technology to teach Hebrew: audiotapes, videotapes, computer tutors. Try these to supplement traditional classes.

Most rabbis want you to know at least some Hebrew before you convert. More importantly, you'll feel better about the conversion if you know at least some.

Q. If I convert, can I stay in touch with my birth family or do I need to break from them?

Epstein. Judaism is not a cruel religion. You can, and should, stay in touch with your birth family. Your memory will not be erased. Your feelings of love and attachment will not disappear.

It is a common conception within Judaism that your conversion is very similar to a rebirth. In a sense you get to start life over. Therefore, the psychological elements of this new life are balanced against the memories of the old to forge a new identity. No part of that new identity includes permanently disregarding your birth family.

Q. What happens at an Introduction to Judaism or conversion class?

Epstein. Of course, classes vary greatly, so you will need to contact a local synagogue or Jewish Community Center about available classes. The time and length of classes also differ. Still, there is often a core curriculum covered in them that might include material on such subjects as God, the Bible, Jewish sacred literature, Jewish terminology, Hebrew, Jewish holidays, Jewish history, synagogue rituals and prayers, the Sabbath, dietary laws, Judaism and other religions, the Jewish life cycle (birth, marriage, death, and so on), anti-Semitism (including the Holocaust), Zionism and

Israel, Jewish parenting, American Judaism, the history of conversion to Judaism, and the laws of conversion. Most classes do not cover all of this material.

Classes are also an opportunity for you to ask questions. It is crucial to ask even the toughest questions you have. I remember one teacher telling students that "The only silly question is the one that remains unasked." Judaism encourages careful scrutiny of ideas. Your asking questions about Judaism is part of your learning to be Jewish.

Q. I don't think I want to convert. Can I still take an Introduction to Judaism class to study Judaism?

Epstein. Yes, you can. Even if you want to convert at the beginning of the class, you may decide ultimately not to do so. Conversion, after all, is a profoundly serious decision. You are not obliged to convert simply by taking the class. I frequently encourage skeptics to take such a course for no other reason than they will enjoy the material and the sorts of questions discussed. Many are surprised to find how much Judaism coheres with what they already believe or helps them put into words unarticulated theological ideas. In either case, taking the course involves no commitment and therefore no risk. That is why I recommend it.

Q. If I finish a conversion class can I change my mind or do I then have to convert?

Epstein. You can change your mind. There is a normal period of doubt. I suppose it's like a case of nervousness before a wedding. When you are about to make a major life change, it is understandable to have some doubts and concerns. Judaism does not ever force anyone to become Jewish. Up until the final step (the particular step will vary depending on the movement you join), you can choose not to become Jewish.

Q. How do I find an Introduction to Judaism class near me?

Epstein. Check with a local synagogue, Jewish Community Center, or other Jewish institution. A list of seventy rabbis who offer classes is at the Conversion to Judaism Home Page, as previously mentioned.

Q. What are the different religious movements within Judaism?

Epstein. The major movements are, in alphabetical order, Conservative, Orthodox, Reconstructionist, and Reform. There are substantial differences among them, which will be discussed in the next question. Many American Jews are secular and do not join a particular movement. Others are more religious but not affiliated currently with one of the movements. I strongly advocate belonging to one of the movements, especially if you are new to Judaism. Having a synagogue gives a person a spiritual home away from home, a prayer community, a constant source of information and support, and a network of contacts, especially with a rabbi. Which movement you join will depend on the circumstances of your life and your own views.

Q. How do I choose which movement to join?

Epstein. One of the real difficulties experienced by people who become Jewish is deciding which movement within Judaism to join. In general, there are four major movements, although there are other, much smaller, groups as well, and some Jews do not affiliate with any group at all. This section includes information about those four major groups. In alphabetical order, the groups are: Conservative, Orthodox, Reconstructionist, and Reform.

It is very difficult to generalize about these groups, and there is great variety within each of the movements. Therefore, the best step for a potential convert to take is to read about each of the groups that sound interesting and, especially, talk with officials of the movement, and visit a local synagogue of that group to attend a service. The descriptions below are not official statements of the respective movements and therefore constitute only my own understanding of them. I suggest contacting the movements directly to get both official statements and guidelines on conversion.

Conservative Judaism

Conservative Judaism is, along with Reform Judaism, one of the two largest Jewish movements. Conservative Jews make up about 40 to 45 percent of those Jews who affiliate. Conservative Judaism accepts the notion that Jewish law (*halachah*) is binding upon Jews. That is, Conservative Jews have an obligation to obey all the teachings (*mitzvot*, which is also translated as 'commandments') of Judaism. Thus, for example, Conservative Jews emphasize the laws of keeping the Sabbath and keeping kosher. Conservative Jews believe that Jewish law, by its very nature, is capable of evolution as humans learn more about interpreting the Torah (the first five Books of the Hebrew Bible). Therefore, Conservative Jews have changed some of the earlier interpretations. For example, men and women worship together in Conservative synagogues, people may ride in a car on the Sabbath to attend services, and women can be ordained as rabbis.

In practice, many Conservative Jews are lax about observing all the religious laws, or obey them only in part. In general, there is a considerable amount of Hebrew in the synagogue services. Conservative Judaism is often seen, perhaps unfairly, as the middle ground between Orthodoxy on its right and Reform and Reconstructionism on its left.

Conservative rabbis will not perform or attend an intermarriage, that is, a marriage between someone born Jewish and an unconverted Gentile. A marriage between a born Jew and a born Gentile who has converted to Judaism is a Jewish marriage and not an intermarriage, and so a Conservative rabbi will perform such a marriage. Conservative rabbis require a male convert to undergo a circumcision or a ceremony of drawing a drop of blood if a circumcision has already been performed, immersion in a ritual bath, and appearance before a religious court. Women converts must also be immersed in a ritual bath and appear before a religious court (see Chapter 7, "The Conversion Process," for further details). Conservative rabbis generally recognize the conversions performed by other rabbis as long as these ritualistic requirements have been met.

There is not one online site for the whole of Conservative Judaism. Like other movements, Conservative Judaism is made up of various organizations, including, for example, the Rabbinical Assembly, the organization of Conservative Rabbis and United Synagogue of Conservative Judaism (http://shamash.org/uscj/), which is the association of Conservative congregations. The major rabbinical seminary for the movement is the Jewish Theological Seminary (http://www.jtsa.edu).

Orthodox Judaism

Orthodox Judaism is a relatively small movement, making up about 10 percent of those Jews who affiliate. Orthodox Jews accept the *halachah* but, unlike Conservative Jews, Orthodox Jews do not believe that the *halachah* itself can evolve. Orthodoxy accepts the idea that the 613 *mitzvot* in the Torah are binding on all Jews. They believe that God literally gave the Torah to Moses and therefore its rules are divine and must be obeyed. Because of this, the Orthodox are the most traditional of Jewish groups. There is often a physical barrier between men and women at services. There are no Orthodox women rabbis. In practice, Orthodox Jews tend to observe Jewish law on such matters as keeping the Sabbath and keeping kosher.

The Orthodox requirements for conversion are the same as those for Conservative Judaism. The crucial difference is that Orthodox rabbis generally do not recognize conversions performed by non-Orthodox rabbis. This fact has caused considerable friction within the Jewish community, and it is important for potential converts to be aware of the problem. The difficulty arises in limited cases. Here is an example: A born Gentile mother was converted by a non-Orthodox rabbi and is married to a Jewish man. Their children, raised as Jews, considered by their community to be Jews, are not considered Jewish by Orthodox rabbis. (The children of Jewish mothers are considered Jewish.) Therefore, if any of those children wanted to marry someone Orthodox, an Orthodox rabbi would refuse to perform the marriage without an Orthodox conversion. A related problem may also arise if the convert or child of a born Gentile mother wishes to immigrate to Israel. The nature of this problem rests on Israeli law at the time of the immigration. Currently, Orthodox Judaism is the only officially recognized movement in Israel for a variety of activities, such as marriage. Orthodox rabbis will not perform or attend an intermarriage.

There are many different Orthodox organizations, with very different practical approaches. The Union of Orthodox Jewish Congregations (http://www.ou.org) is a major one.

Reconstructionist Judaism

Reconstructionist Jews are a small segment of American Jews, perhaps 3 percent of those who affiliate. However, Reconstructionism has made intellectual contributions to Jewish life that transcend its small numbers. Reconstructionists believe in a naturalistic approach to religion and conceive of Judaism not just as a religion but as an evolving religious civilization. They do not accept the binding nature of Jewish law and reject the notion of Jews as a chosen people. In general, Reconstructionism tends to be the most liberal of the Jewish movements in many areas. For further information, contact the Jewish Reconstructionist Federation (http://shamash.org/jrf/).

Reform Judaism

Reform Jews make up what is probably the largest group of American Jews who are affiliated—about 45 percent of American Jews.

Reform Jews do not accept the binding nature of Jewish law, focusing instead on the moral autonomy of individuals to decide which laws are religiously meaningful for them. In general, Reform Judaism is a liberal religious movement whose adherents often support liberal social causes. Generally, the Reform service has less Hebrew than do the Orthodox or Conservative services. The Reform movement is often thought, sometimes by its own members, to be the most lenient when it comes to religious practices. For example, keeping kosher is not required. However, there is some movement in contemporary Reform practices back toward embracing some of the traditional ones.

Reform Judaism, like Reconstructionism, believes that children of a Jewish father and Gentile mother are Jewish if the child is brought up as Jewish and publicly identifies as a Jew through various religious acts. That is, for Reform Jews, such a child need not convert in order to be Jewish. This idea, called patrilineality, is opposed by the Conservative and Orthodox movements, which do not recognize those children as Jewish. They follow the matrilineal principle that a person is Jewish if that person's mother is Jewish or if that person converts to Judaism. The potential for problems here is obvious.

Reform Jews have the largest number of converts and the largest number of intermarried families of all the movements. The movement has formed an effective outreach program for intermarried families.

There is further information online about the organizations within the Reform movement (http://www.shamash.org/reform/).

Q. Do the members of each movement recognize conversions from other movements?

Epstein. This question can only be answered in very general terms. In general, the Reconstructionist and Reform movements recognize conversions performed by rabbis of all the movements. The Orthodox movement, in general, does not recognize conversions performed by non-Orthodox rabbis, or even by Orthodox rabbis, if the process was not done correctly. The Conservative movement generally recognizes conversions performed by the Orthodox movement. It also recognizes conversions performed by the Reform and Reconstructionist movements depending on the conversion process. For example, if a circumcision, immersion in a ritual bath, and other requirements are met, then the conversion is recognized by the Conservatives. For an up-to-date status report, consult your local rabbi.

Q. What conversions are accepted in Israel?

Epstein. Generally speaking, Orthodox conversions are accepted in Israel. No non-Orthodox conversions performed in Israel are accepted as of the time of this writing. Non-Orthodox conversions performed outside Israel are accepted as far as the Law of Return. (This law permits Jews to immigrate to Israel and receive citizenship immediately.) More than any other issue discussed in the book, this situation can change. Please check with a local rabbi for an up-to-date report.

Q. How can I contact a rabbi?

Epstein. Check with a friend or local Board of Rabbis. If you are on a college campus, you can check with a campus Jewish organization, such as Hillel. Be careful in looking up rabbis in the phone book that the "rabbi" is not a Hebrew Christian. You should also determine what movement the rabbi belongs to.

Q. What questions will the rabbi ask me at our first meeting?

Epstein. A first meeting is a time for both of you to get to know each other. The rabbi will be interested in your religious background, that is, the religion, if any, of your parents, your religious education, and your feelings about your birth religion now. You will, of course, also be asked about why you wish to convert. This question is an important one in Jewish life, because many rabbis view the motive for your conversion as crucial. The rabbi may be concerned that your motivations arise from a bad reason, such as emotional pressure from a partner or fear of losing the partner if you do not convert. More genuine reasons, such as a love of Judaism, are seen as appropriate. There is a difference of opinion among some very traditional rabbis and others about what in Jewish law constitutes a legal reason for a conversion. Some think a romantic interest, or concern for family, is a beginning motive that can lead to love of Judaism. A few remain concerned that such motives are not sufficient. I think it is fair to say that the vast majority of rabbis, recognizing that conversion is not required to get married, now believe that the very desire to convert is a sign of sincerity. At any rate, before seeing the rabbi it is important for you to examine, understand, and be able to articulate the reasons that you wish to become Jewish.

The rabbi might also ask other questions of your personal status, such as whether you are married or have ever been married, the religion of your partner, whether you have children, and so on.

Other questions will include your knowledge of Judaism. What do you already know about Jewish beliefs and practices? Can you truly accept the basic and crucial differences between Judaism and your birth religion? What experiences with Jews and Jewish life have you had? Was it your decision, without being pressured, to become Jewish? Are you willing to spend the necessary time studying in class and at home to become Jewish? The reason this is asked is that an Introduction to Judaism class can take six months or longer depending on the movement, your background, and your rabbi's specific requirements.

The rabbi will also ask if you have discussed this decision with your birth family, and, if married, with your marriage family. The rabbi will certainly want to determine that if you convert you will want to raise your children in the Jewish faith.

Finally, the rabbi will ask if you have any questions. Be sure you ask as many questions as you wish in order to feel comfortable. Certainly don't worry about asking a "silly" or "dumb" question. If a question is on your mind, ask it. Rabbis are specialists in responding to your questions.

6
Judaism and Christianity

Q. Can I be both Jewish and Christian?

Epstein. Judaism has great respect for Christianity. Part of that respect involves not blurring the genuine lines between them. No mainstream Jewish movement recognizes the possibility that a person can be Jewish while believing in Jesus as the Messiah or in any way professing Christian religious views.

There are religious movements that fall under the general heading of Hebrew Christians. These movements claim to be both Jewish and Christian; indeed, they claim that their followers are "completed" Jews by having accepted Jesus. It is certainly legitimate for Christians to investigate the Jewish origins of their religion, and they are, of course, entitled to their beliefs. However, their desire to be accepted as legitimate Jews has not been accepted, or even considered, because their views are fully Christian and, because of that, incapable of simultaneously being Jewish. Put simply, if one believes in Jesus as the Messiah, then one cannot be Jewish. A person with those beliefs is seen by the Jewish community as a Christian.

Q. How does Judaism differ from Christianity? For example, what do Jews think about Jesus?

Epstein. There are many substantial and vital distinctions between Judaism and Christianity. Of course, there are many similarities as well, primarily because Christianity emerged from Judaism. However, the emergence was not a direct line. Christianity broke from Judaism, forming a new religion, and so it is misleading, however comfortable the thought might be, to believe that the two religions are essentially the same, or to see Christianity as the natural continuation of Judaism.

The differences between the two religions will be explored in this response. As a preface, it is useful to repeat Judaism's central belief that the people of all religions are children of God, and therefore equal before God. All people have God's love, mercy, and help. In particular, Judaism does not require that a person convert to Judaism in order to achieve salvation. The only requirement for that, as understood by Jews, is to be ethical. While Judaism accepts the worth of all people regardless of religion, it also allows people who are not Jewish but who voluntarily wish to join the Jewish people to do so.

It is not really possible to summarize either Judaism or Christianity fairly in this section, so further study is encouraged. Also, the formal positions of Judaism on various issues should be discussed with a rabbi. The beliefs described in this section are mainstream Christian and Jewish beliefs. Individual Christian and Jewish thinkers may differ, sometimes considerably, with the positions described here. It is nonetheless useful, even with all these limitations, to consider the differences. One book that is excellent on this subject is *Judaism and Christianity: The Differences*, by Trude Weiss-Rosmarin (Queens, NY: Jonathan David, 1981).

God

Judaism insists on a notion of monotheism, the idea that there is one God. As Judaism understands this idea, God cannot be made up of parts, even if those parts are mysteriously united. The Christian notion of trinitarianism is that God is made up of God the Father, God the Son, and God the Holy Spirit. Such a view, even if called monotheistic because the three parts are, by divine mystery, only one God, is incompatible with the Jewish view that such a division is not possible. The most fundamental Jewish idea is that God is one. This idea allows for God's unity and uniqueness as a creative force. Thus, for Jews, God is the creator of all that we like and all that we don't. There is no evil force with an ability to create equal to God's. Judaism sees Christianity's trinitarianism as a weakening of the idea of God's oneness. Jews do not have a set group of beliefs about the nature of God; therefore, there is considerable, and approved, debate within Judaism about God. However, all mainstream Jewish groups reject the idea of God's having three parts. Indeed, many Jews see an attempt to divide God as a partial throwback, or compromise with, the pagan conception of many gods.

The Jewish View of Jesus

To Christians, the central tenet of their religion is the belief that Jesus is the Son of God, part of the trinity, the savior of souls who is the messiah. He is God's revelation through flesh. Jesus was, in Christian terms, God incarnate, God in the flesh who came to Earth to absorb the sins of humans and therefore free from sin those who accepted his divinity.

To Jews, whatever wonderful teacher and storyteller Jesus may have been, he was just a human, not the son of God (except in the metaphorical sense in which all humans are children of God). In the Jewish view, Jesus cannot save souls; only God can. Jesus did not, in the Jewish view, rise from the dead.

He also did not absorb the sins of people. For Jews, sins are removed not by Jesus's atonement but by seeking forgiveness. Jews seek forgiveness from God for sins against God, and from other people (not just God) for sins against those people. Seeking forgiveness requires a sincere sense of repentance but also seeking directly to redress the wrong done to someone. Sins are partially removed through prayer, which replaced animal sacrifice as a way of relieving sins. They are also removed by correcting errors against others.

Jesus, for Christians, replaced Jewish law. For traditional Jews, the commandments (*mitzvot*) and Jewish law (*halachah*) are still binding.

Jesus is not seen as the messiah. In the Jewish view, the messiah is a human being who will usher in an era of peace. We can tell the messiah by looking at the world and seeing if it is at peace. From the Jewish view, this clearly did not happen when Jesus was on Earth or anytime after his death.

Jews vary about what they think of Jesus as a man. Some respect him as an ethical teacher who accepted Jewish law, as someone who didn't even see himself as the messiah, who didn't want to start a new religion at all. Rather, Jesus is seen by these Jews as someone who challenged the religious authorities of his day for their practices. In this view, he meant to improve Judaism according to his own understanding, not to break with it. Whatever the Jewish response is, one point is crucial. No one who is Jewish, no born Jew and no one who converts to Judaism, can believe in Jesus as the literal son of God or as the messiah. For the Jewish people, there is no God but God.

Free Will and Original Sin

Judaism does not accept the notion of original sin, the idea that people are bad from birth and cannot remove sin by themselves but need an act of grace provided by the sacrificial death of Jesus as atonement for all of humanity's sins. For Christians, there are no other forms of salvation other than through Jesus.

In contrast, the Jewish view is that humans are not born naturally good or naturally bad. They have both a good and a bad inclination in them, but they have the free moral will to choose the good, and this free moral will can be more powerful than the evil inclination. Indeed, Jewish ethics requires the idea that humans decide for themselves how to act. This is so because temptation, and with it the possibility of sin, allows people to choose good and thus have moral merit. The Jewish view is not that humans are helpless in the face of moral error.

Death, Heaven, and Hell

In general, Jewish thinkers have focused on the ways to lead a good life on Earth and improve this world, leaving concerns about death and beyond until the appropriate time. Judaism has stressed the natural fact of death and its role in giving life meaning. Of course, issues of death are inevitably important. The fear of death, concern about the fate of our own soul and those of our loved ones, ethical concerns that some people die unfairly—all these and many other issues are discussed in Jewish literature. Since God is seen as ultimately just, the seeming injustice on Earth has propelled many traditional Jewish thinkers into seeing the afterlife as a way to reflect the ultimate justice of human existence.

Traditional thinkers have considered how individuals would be rewarded or punished after their deaths. There are a few rare descriptions of life after death. Traditionalists gave the name Gehenna to the place where souls were punished. Many Jewish thinkers noted that since, essentially, God is filled with mercy and love, punishment is not to be considered to be eternal. There are, similarly, many varying conceptions of paradise, such as that paradise is the place where we finally understand the true concept of God. It is also possible that there is no separate Heaven and Hell, only lesser or greater distance from God after death. In addition, punishment might be self-determined on the basis of suffering in kind the suffering the person brought about. That is, Judaism doesn't have a clear sense of Heaven and Hell, with different places in Hell for different punishments. Rather, the idea is that God uses the afterlife to provide ultimate justice and for the wicked to seek some sort of final redemption.

Judaism does not believe that people who are Gentiles will automatically go to Hell or that Jews will automatically go to Heaven just on the basis of their belonging to the faith. Rather, individual ethical behavior is what is most important. Many traditional Jews believe that Judaism provides the best guide to leading such an ethical life.

Q. Do Jews try to convert Christians?

Epstein. No. Jews accept that believing Christians who act morally can find God through their own religion. Within Judaism, there is not a claim that Judaism is the sole path to Heaven and nonbelievers (that is, non-Jews) will burn in Hell. Therefore, there is no theological reason to seek converts among Christians.

Also, for millennia Jews have suffered persecution, often at the hands of Christians who sought, by force and other means, to make Jews convert to Christianity. Jews thought that was morally abhorrent and so do not wish to be guilty of similar acts.

It is not uncommon for a rabbi to try to convince a potential convert to examine his or her birth religion as a pathway to God.

Judaism does not "target" any religious or ethnic group, or anyone else as a potential convert. Rather, Judaism simply remains open and welcoming to those who, on their own, wish to join the Jewish people.

Q. Why are Jews opposed to Christians who try to convert Jews?

Epstein. Jews believe that all adherents of the monotheistic religions can reach God. Just as Jews do not try to convert others, Jews do not want to be the target of conversion efforts. The legacy of the hatred of Jews, which across history has resulted in the deaths and forced conversions of untold millions of Jews, is a powerful part of Jewish consciousness. Given this history, any attempt to convert Jews is viewed at some level as anti-Jewish. In addition, Jews are an endangered people. Any diminution of its numbers means, in terms of percentage, a much greater loss, say, than the conversion of a Christian.

7
The Conversion Process

Q. What are the steps in the conversion process?

Epstein. The steps to a conversion vary, sometimes to a great degree, according to the movement joined and, to some extent, the rabbi with whom one studies. Here is a general outline. I've tried to include all possible steps. As always, for a definitive decision about the process for you, you need to discuss your conversion with a rabbi.

Here, then, are some common steps:

1. Considering Judaism

The conversion process begins when a person considers the possibility of becoming Jewish. The reasons why people become Jewish are varied. Many are involved in a romantic relationship with someone Jewish and wish to unite the family religiously. Others are on a spiritual search and learn about Judaism through such means as reading, hearing a lecture, attending a Jewish religious ceremony, and so on. Whatever the motivation, the first step in considering conversion is to explore Judaism. This early exploration might include discussing the subject with friends and family, taking out books and videos on Judaism, or just thinking about whether conversion is the right choice.

2. Finding a Rabbi

If, after the initial consideration, a person wishes to explore conversion more fully, the next step is to find a rabbi. This part of the process can be difficult for several reasons. Obviously, individual rabbis differ. Some devote more time than others to conversion candidates. Some adhere to an ancient tradition of turning away a candidate three times to test the candidate's sincerity. In general, though, rabbis are extremely dedicated people who are both intelligent and religiously sensitive. They are Judaism's gatekeepers. They decide who can enter into Judaism. Given their central importance to a potential convert, it makes sense to visit several rabbis and several synagogues to look for a compatible match.

If you are looking for a rabbi, check with friends and family for advice. Contact a local board of rabbis or other Jewish group, or check a local telephone directory. You can also contact the movements directly.

A second problem is that rabbis belong to different groupings or movements. The four major movements are Conservative, Orthodox, Reconstructionist, and Reform Judaism. It is important for potential candidates to understand the differences among these movements and choose which movement is right for them.

When a person does see a rabbi, the rabbi can authoritatively answer questions about conversion. If the person has already decided to convert, the rabbi will probably ask a series of questions about that decision. Such questions might include some of these:

> Why do you want to convert?
> What is your religious background?
> What do you know about Judaism?
> Do you know the differences between Judaism and your birth
> religion?

Were you pressured to convert?

Are you willing to spend the necessary time studying to become Jewish?

Are you willing to raise any children you might have as Jewish?

Have you discussed this decision with your family?

Do you have any questions about Judaism or conversion?

3. Learning Judaism

A decision has been made to study Judaism, and a rabbi has agreed to oversee that studying. A person might not yet be fully sure that a conversion is right, but the initial steps of exploration will continue. Even those who don't ultimately convert generally find that studying Judaism is both interesting and helpful in making a final decision about conversion.

Converts study Judaism in a variety of ways. Some work directly with a rabbi, meeting regularly and fulfilling specific study assignments. Others attend formal Introduction to Judaism or conversion classes, often with their Jewish romantic partner. A typical course of study will include basic Jewish beliefs and religious practices, such as prayer services, the history of the Jewish people, the Jewish home, the Jewish holidays and life cycle, the Holocaust, and Israel, as well as other topics. The study of Hebrew is also included.

The period of study varies greatly. In general, the range is from six months to a year, although there are variations. Many Gentiles preparing to marry someone Jewish go through this process early so as to get married in a Jewish ceremony. A marriage between someone born Jewish and someone who becomes Jewish is a Jewish marriage, not an intermarriage. If this is a crucial issue, plan to begin study well before a wedding.

Usually during this study period, a rabbi will ask that the person begin practicing Judaism according to the understanding of the movement. This can be a worthwhile time to explore Judaism. For example, even if a person does not ultimately plan to keep kosher (observe Jewish ritual rules about food), it is valuable to explore the rules for keeping kosher during this period of study.

4. The Religious Court

The Religious Court, or *Bet Din*, most often consists of three people, at least one of whom must be a rabbi. Often it consists of three rabbis. The *Bet Din* officially oversees the formal conversion. Individual rabbis will provide guidance about how the *Bet Din* works. Because it takes place after learning, one part of the conversion candidate's appearance will be to determine the candidate's Jewish knowledge. There might, for example, be a question about the meaning of the Jewish Sabbath or about the Jewish belief in one God. These questions are not meant to trap candidates. Obviously, candidates are nervous during such questioning, but in almost all cases the questions are simply meant to assess the sincerity of the candidate and to make sure the conversion was entered into freely. Often an oath of allegiance to the Jewish people is made.

5. Circumcision

The specific requirements for conversion and their order need to be discussed with a rabbi. One requirement for males who wish to be converted by an Orthodox or Conservative rabbi is circumcision, or *brit milah*. If a circumcision has already been performed, the Orthodox and Conservative movements require that a drop of blood be drawn as a symbolic circumcision. This ceremony is called *Hatafat Dam Brit*. The Reform and Reconstructionist movements generally do not require a circumcision as part of the conversion process.

6. Immersion

Orthodox and Conservative rabbis require both male and female conversion candidates to immerse themselves in a ritual bath called a *mikvah*. This ceremony is called *tevilah*. Reform and

Reconstructionist rabbis generally do not require the use of a *mikvah*, but some highly recommend it. The *mikvah* can be any body of natural water, although the term usually refers to a specific pool that is built for the purposes of ritual purification. The equipment used varies according to the *mikvah*. The immersion ceremony usually starts with cleaning the body as by a shower. The person is covered and the covering removed as the person enters the warm *mikvah* waters, which are usually about 4 feet deep. (When the ceremony is done in a public place such as a lake the candidate wears a loose-fitting garment.) Blessings are recited, and the person then bends into the water. According to traditional Jewish law, three male witnesses must be present, although this rule has been reinterpreted so that, in some movements, Jewish females can be witnesses. When there are male witnesses and the candidate is female, the witnesses wait outside the *mikvah* room and are told by a female attendant that the immersion has been completed and the blessings recited.

7. The Offering

In ancient times, conversion candidates brought sacrifices or offerings to the Temple in Jerusalem. After the Temple was destroyed, this ceremony disappeared. Jewish law therefore does not require such an offering, however, some rabbis, especially among the Orthodox, mention it as an opportunity to engage in an act of donating money to the poor or another act of charity to make a symbolic offering. This step can voluntarily be added to the conversion process.

8. Choosing a Name

Again, particular conversion processes will vary. Frequently, after a *bet din* and the signing of an oath, a Hebrew name is chosen. This is then followed by a visit to a *mikvah*. At any rate, at some point, you will be asked to pick a Hebrew name. By tradition, male converts choose the Hebrew name Avraham as their new Hebrew first name and female candidates traditionally choose Sarah or Ruth. Since the use of Hebrew names includes mention of the parents' Hebrew names, and the convert has no Jewish parents, traditionalists add *ben Avraham Avinu*, or son of Abraham, our Father. Therefore if a male chooses the Hebrew name Avraham, that male's full Hebrew name would be Avraham ben Avraham Avinu. For women, the addition is *bat Sarah Imenu*, daughter of Sarah, our Mother. The naming ceremony includes a blessing.

9. The Public Ceremony

A public ceremony announcing the conversion is becoming more popular, especially among Reform Jews. This ceremony usually involves the convert standing in front of the congregation and giving a speech, most typically about the reasons for converting or the lessons learned through the conversion experience.

10. A Special Case: The Conversion of Minors

Minors can be converted. In families with a non-Jewish mother and a Jewish father, the child is considered Jewish by the Reform movement if the child is brought up engaging in public acts of identification with Judaism. Orthodox and Conservative Judaism, however, do not regard such a child as legally Jewish. Therefore, parents of such children frequently have their children converted in infancy because the process is quite simple. Reform rabbis often simply have a naming ceremony. Orthodox and Conservative rabbis require the *mikvah* for a female minor and a circumcision and *mikvah* for a male minor.

Q. I'm afraid to contact a rabbi. What should I do?

Epstein. The word *rabbi* means 'teacher'. In Judaism, a rabbi is not an intermediary between God and humans but simply a very learned person. We admire rabbis because they have studied the sacred texts of Judaism and work to improve Jewish life, not because they are somehow closer to God. Still, rabbis are clearly the key people in a person's conversion and, therefore, can be intimidating. My suggestion is to ask as many people as you can for advice about speaking with a rabbi. You can go online at my web site and e-mail some rabbis anonymously if you wish.

While rabbis are extremely busy people, almost all will take the time to meet and speak with you.

It is also all right to have someone contact a rabbi first. Once in a while, someone asks me to do that, and I always am glad to do so or to help in some way to put the person in touch with a rabbi.

If you are on a college campus, check with Hillel or another Jewish organization.

You can get additional information about rabbis and conversion from the major religious groupings within Judaism:

Conservative Movement

The Rabbinical Assembly (the organization of rabbis affiliated with the Conservative movement) and the United Synagogue of Conservative Judaism (the organization of Conservative congregations) have established a Joint Commission on Intermarriage. Part of the purpose of this Commission is to make the option of conversion to Judaism more widely known among those in interfaith marriages in which one partner is Jewish. The Commission has a variety of written materials on conversion to Judaism, including two volumes by Rabbi Alan Silverstein, Ph.D., who is a Co-Chair of the Commission. The contact person for the Commission is Rabbi Jan C. Kaufman. Rabbi Kaufman's address is:

The Rabbinical Assembly
3080 Broadway
New York, NY 10027
(212) 678-8060

Orthodox Movement

Contact:

RCA Commission on Gerut
Rabbinical Council of America
305 Seventh Avenue
New York, NY 10001
(212) 807-9042

Reconstructionist Movement

Contact:

RRA Commission on Gerut
Reconstructionist Rabbinical Association
Church Road and Greenwood Avenue
Wyncote, PA 19095
(215) 576-5210

Reform Movement

The Union of American Hebrew Congregations (the organization of congregations affiliated with the Reform movement) and the Central Conference of American Rabbis (the organization of Reform rabbis) established the Commission on Reform Jewish Outreach. This Commission has an extensive list of publications and various regional outreach staff across the United States. In addition, the Commission has established the *Reform Jewish Outreach Home Page* (URL: http://shamash.org/reform/uahc/outreach).

For further information, contact Dru Greenwood, the Commission's Director:

Commission on Reform Jewish Outreach
UAHC
838 Fifth Avenue

New York, NY 10021
(212) 249-0100

Q. I'm a male. Do I need a circumcision in order to convert?

Epstein. Orthodox and Conservative rabbis require a circumcision if you have not already had one. Some Reform rabbis require it; most do not.

In Hebrew, a circumcision is called a *Brit Milah*, and the person who performs it is called a *mohel* (pronounced "moyl"). It is not simply a medical or health procedure. A *brit* is a covenant or formal agreement. For example, by tradition the Jewish people entered into a brit at Mt. Sinai with God. Abraham, in the Bible, formally entered into a covenant with God by the act of circumcision. There is a tradition that Abraham was 99 when his circumcision took place so that nobody could claim to be too old to have a circumcision. Thus, traditional Judaism sees such an act as a serious statement of willingness to enter the covenant.

The traditional service involving circumcision is very brief. A brief blessing is said prior to the circumcision and two longer blessings afterward accompanied with a cup of wine.

Q. If I've already had a circumcision, do I need another one?

Epstein. Some males are born without a foreskin, and some have had a circumcision (the typical case is as an infant for health reasons). Orthodox and Conservative rabbis require that a drop of blood be drawn as a symbolic circumcision. This ceremony is called a *Hatafat Dam Brit*.

There may also be male candidates with particular medical and psychological circumstances. These people will need to consult a rabbi.

Q. Why do some rabbis allow conversion without circumcision?

Epstein. Orthodox and Conservative rabbis may allow it if circumcision could be a life-threatening procedure. This is determined on a case-by-case basis.

Reform and Reconstructionist rabbis who do not require circumcision have individual reasons for doing so. The ones I have spoken with usually cite the difficulty of an adult undergoing the procedure. Note that Orthodox and Conservative rabbis will generally not recognize a conversion if it does not include circumcision for a male.

Q. I'm scared about getting a circumcision. Any suggestions?

Epstein. Read about it. Talk to the *mohel* who will perform the ceremony. Speak to others who have undergone it. Think of it not as a medical but as a religious act to get closer to God. Men may have a general fear of surgery and question the effect of such surgery on their masculinity. Of course, it is crucial to understand that for Judaism to make this a central component of its religious life, ordinary males would not suffer any physical damage or experience any lasting psychological damage. Ultimately, the decision about circumcision becomes a personal one. If a male does wish to convert with an Orthodox or Conservative rabbi, a circumcision or *hatafat dam brit* is required.

Q. What is a *bet din*?

Epstein. A *bet din* is a religious court made up of three people. Sometimes all three are rabbis. In all cases, they are learned people who know about conversion. Most rabbis in all denominations will require that a conversion candidate appear before a *bet din* at the end of the learning process. Some rabbis also want an appearance at a *bet din* at the conversion ceremony.

In many cases, especially among Reform and Conservative Jews, a convert's Jewish romantic partner may be in attendance at the *bet din*.

A *bet din* serves various purposes. Because it will occur after a process of learning about Judaism, the *bet din* will want to test the applicant's basic knowledge of Judaism. The questions, of course, vary, but they will have been covered in a course of study. They may, for example, include questions about Jewish holidays, the Jewish home, the meaning of the Sabbath, the idea of the unity of God, and so on. These are not trick questions; no one will ask what's in the footnote on page 43 of a book you have read. These will be serious, thoughtful questions. They may, in fact, be more general, such as asking why you want to be Jewish. Members of a *bet din* are used to people being nervous.

In addition to testing some knowledge, the *bet din* will want to make sure that your choice to enter Judaism is freely made and is not being done only because of emotional pressure to convert. A conversion must be the choice of the candidate.

Candidates might be asked about their feelings about leaving their birth religion. They might be asked if they are ready to cast their lot with the Jewish people, to identify their fate and the fate of their family and their future descendants with a people that has suffered persecution. Often an oath of allegiance to the Jewish people is officially signed.

Q. What questions will a *bet din* ask me?

Epstein. See the previous question for a general overview. The best way to prepare is to go over materials from the course of study you took, discuss any questions with your rabbi, prepare to explain why you are becoming Jewish, and think through what you might say when asked about your feelings toward your birth religion.

It might help to talk to others who have been through the experience. Everyone I have spoken with has told me they enjoyed the *bet din* even though they were a bit nervous. It gave them an opportunity to discuss all that they had learned.

Q. What is a *mikvah*?

Epstein. Both Orthodox and Conservative rabbis have as a conversion requirement that both female and male candidates for conversion immerse themselves in a *mikvah*, or ritual bath. The ceremony of immersion is called *tevilah*. While many Reform rabbis may not require their conversion candidates to enter a *mikvah*, many recommend it. After speaking with many converts, I have come to the conclusion that, if possible, and if your rabbi approves, you should request a *mikvah* experience even if it is not required. Many people have told me they found entering the *mikvah* one of the most moving parts of their conversion experience; it made them find a specific moment during which they felt reborn as a Jew. Indeed, entering the *mikvah* is supposed to render a person ritually clean and ready to become Jewish.

In fact, any body of natural water can serve as a *mikvah*. Such bodies as a lake, an ocean, or any other natural waters are legally accepted. Many Conservative rabbis also allow, when necessary, a swimming pool to function as a *mikvah*. More traditionally, a *mikvah* is a special pool that is specifically built for the purposes of providing ritual cleanliness. Such a *mikvah* might be located in a house of worship or Jewish Community Center, or in a separate building. Actually, there are precise requirements regarding a *mikvah* that are adhered to by traditional rabbis. According to traditional Jewish law, a *mikvah* has to be built into either the ground or a building's structure and must have at least 200 gallons (24 cubic feet) of water. Because the water had to be brought to the *mikvah* in a natural way, you might see cement channels on the *mikvah* roof's sides. This allows rainwater to flow to the *mikvah* directly. Later, when this is done, waters brought in by pipes can be added.

Some modern *mikvah*s are well-equipped; some even have hair dryers.

Different *mikvah*s may have different appearances.

Q. What am I supposed to do in a *mikvah*?

Epstein. The conversion candidate can bring along a Jewish friend or partner. Traditional law requires that the ceremony occur during daylight hours and on a weekday. (This is true not just for a *mikvah* ceremony but for all other activities of a Jewish court.)

Usually, the process in a *mikvah* goes like this: The conversion candidate prepares for the ritual immersion by making sure the body is thoroughly clean. This is an important point. The *mikvah* is for an already clean body to make it holy. This cleanliness is achieved, typically, by a simple shower. A *mikvah* often has shower facilities. For women candidates, the scheduling of *mikvah* is important in that traditional rabbis will want to schedule it after a period (judged to be five days or after the menstrual blood has disappeared).

A candidate wears a covering over the body that is removed when the candidate goes into the water. The water is usually warm, and four feet is a common depth. Of course, if the *mikvah* being used is not a private one but a public one, such as a natural body of water, the garment can be worn as long as it fits loosely.

A common method for the immersion is to have the candidate stand with his or her legs apart and arms loose bent over. All the body must be immersed in the water. The body should enter the water all at once. (Traditional rabbis may have the candidate submerge until the water is up to the neck. At that point the *Bet Din* will tell the convert about some important Jewish mitzvot, teachings, or commandments. Then the candidate submerges until the entire body is under water.)

After the person has immersed herself or himself, the candidate says a blessing: *Baruch atta Adonai, Eloheinu melech ha olam, asher kideshanu be mitzvotav vitzivanu al ha tevilah.* This means: 'Blessed are You, Lord our God, Ruler of the universe, who sanctified us through Your teachings and taught us concerning immersion.' (Note: I have translated the word *mitzvot* as 'teachings'; others often translate it as 'commandment'.)

The candidate then submerges two more times. These are followed by the *Shehecheyanu* blessing: *Baruch attah Adonai, Eloheinu melech ha olam, shehecheyanu, vikiyemanu, vehigiyanu la z'man ha zeh.* (This means: 'Blessed are You, Lord our God, Ruler of the universe, who has kept us alive and sustained us, and allowed us to reach this day'.)

When the candidate has completed this blessing, the candidate is then Jewish.

Halachah makes it a requirement that there are three qualified male witnesses to the immersion. To maintain modesty, however, when the conversion candidate is a woman, the male witnesses remain outside the mikveh room and are told by a female attendant that both the immersion is taking place and that the appropriate blessings are being said. In certain cases, Jewish women are used to serve as the witnesses.

Frequently, the moment is celebrated such as with a meal.

Q. I read about an ancient Jewish custom of giving an offering when conversion occurs. What was that and do I have to do it?

Epstein. In ancient times, many religious ceremonies centered on the Temple in Jerusalem. (The Western Wall, which is the holiest site in Judaism, is the only remaining part of the Second Temple. It is a retaining wall, not an original wall of the Temple.) The original Temple, built by Solomon, was destroyed in 586 B.C.E. (meaning Before the Common Era; Jews use B.C.E. instead of B.C., which stands for 'Before Christ' and is obviously a Christian designation). This Temple was rebuilt but was destroyed by the Romans in the year 70 C.E. (meaning Common Era; Jews use C.E. instead of A.D., which means 'Anno Domini' or 'In the Year of our Lord', a Christian designation).

Since then no Temple has been built in Jerusalem. Today, a huge Mosque stands on the site where the Temple was originally built.

A typical religious ceremony was to bring a sacrifice to the Temple. Converts in ancient times adhered to this tradition by bringing either a sacrifice or an offering to the Temple. The conversion candidate actually entered the Temple sanctuary. Of course, after the Roman destruction, making such an offering was no longer possible, although some Jewish scholars maintained that converts should set some offering aside that could be given whenever the Temple is rebuilt. This requirement is not part of Jewish law, however.

Still, to me at least, the notion of giving some offering is useful. Some rabbis are beginning to suggest that this part of the conversion process be done by donating money to the poor or engaging in some comparable form of charity as at least a symbolic offering.

I suggest you consider voluntarily adding this step to your conversion process.

Q. How do I choose a Hebrew name?

Epstein. As is frequently the case in religious matters, different rabbis will handle the exact order of the naming process differently. For males, sometimes it is held at the same time as the circumcision. Often it is completed right after the *mikvah* ceremony. At some point, then, you will have to choose a Hebrew name. This name is important, for you will use it for all future Jewish religious ceremonies, such as a marriage or an aliyah at a Torah reading. (This involves reciting blessings before and after a part of the Torah is read.) Of course, your new name also is symbolic of your spiritual rebirth as a Jew.

In Judaism, a Hebrew name includes mention of parents. Gentile parent names are, obviously, inappropriate as part of a Hebrew name. Because of spiritual rebirth, it is common for converts to be called *ben Avraham Avinu*, or "son of Abraham, our Father" or *bat Sarah Imenu*, "daughter of Sarah, our Mother." Of course, your children need not use this designation; they will use your Hebrew name.

There are many valuable books listing Hebrew names. Some typical ones include, besides Abraham (full name as Avraham ben Avraham Avinu), Yaakov (Jacob), Ruth, Shimon, Naomi, Dov, and many, many others. Consult a Hebrew name dictionary for a large number of choices.

Here is a modern text of the blessing for women. I have made the language gender-neutral and added Sarah's name. The same prayer is said by men with the appropriate linguistic substitutions (note: some rabbis add another prayer as well):

> Our God and God of our Ancestors: Sustain this woman in God's Torah and in God's teachings and may her name in Israel be known as [here the Hebrew name is inserted], daughter of Abraham our Father and Sarah our Mother. May this woman rejoice in the Torah and glory in its teachings. Praise God for God is good and is kind for all eternity. May (name inserted), the daughter of Abraham our Father and Sarah our Mother, grow to become great. May she enter the Lord's Torah, and learn God's teachings and perform good deeds.

Q. Why are so many converts named after Abraham, Sarah, and Ruth?

Epstein. This requires a clarification. Remember that all converts, traditionally, have ben Avraham Avinu or bat Sarah Imenu as part of their Hebrew names. These are preceded by another name, such as Ruth bat Avraham Avinu v' Sarah Imenu. In fact, quite a few converts in medieval and other times did pick a first name of Abraham, so that their full Hebrew name was Avraham ben Avraham Avinu. (Today, we might add Sarah's name as well.) When Abraham (or Avraham, in Hebrew) was picked, it was because Abraham was born a Gentile but was the founder, along with Sarah, of the people eventually known as Jews. It is also the case that Abraham and Sarah "gathered souls," which the rabbis from the Talmudic period interpreted as meaning that the two won converts to their new monotheistic religion.

Ruth, of course, is the most famous convert in the Bible. Ruth, who lived probably sometime in the eleventh century B.C.E., was born a Moabite, a Gentile. She married Mahlon, who was a Hebrew. Mahlon and his father Elimelech, his mother, Naomi, and his brother, Chilian, had originally lived in Bethlehem in the Land of Israel but had to leave because of a famine. The family journeyed to Moab, which then was a land east of the Dead Sea. The fertile highlands in Moab seemed to offer the promise of food. Instead of finding sustenance, however, the family found tragedy. Elimelech, Mahlon, and Chilian all died there.

Naomi and her two daughters-in-law, Ruth and Orpah, were the only members of the family left alive. Naomi was, by then, old and tired. She wished to return to the Land of Israel, where she had been born. Naomi advised both of her daughters-in-law to return to their mothers because both were young enough so that they might remarry. Orpah quickly agreed to do what Naomi advised. Ruth, however, did not follow the advice. She did not see her mother-in-law as a burden to be discarded. Ruth expressed her continuing love for Mahlon, her dead husband, by maintaining her loyalty to his mother, to the people of the Land of Israel, and, finally, to God. When Naomi asked her to leave, Ruth said, "Do not try to persuade me to leave you, to turn back, and not go with you. Wherever you go, I will go too. Wherever you stay, I will stay. Your people shall be my people, and your God my God."

Ruth became the model for converts and the great-grandmother of King David, and thus an ancestor of the Messiah according to Jewish tradition.

Q. What if I want a public ceremony?

Epstein. In some cases, a rabbi will allow some sort of a public or graduation ceremony. Again, you need to check this with the rabbi working with you. Such a ceremony often takes the form of a new convert standing in front of the congregation and giving a speech such as why the person has become Jewish.

Of course, there are many converts who do not wish to have any public recognition. Some feel, with absolute accuracy, that they are now fully Jewish (at least within their movements) and do not wish to be artificially segregated as "converts" but to be accepted as what they actually are, just Jews. Others might like a public ceremony but are shy.

If it is allowed, I suggest that converts accept this challenge. Many of those I have been in contact with recommended it for those undergoing conversion. Such a ceremony, they have pointed out, gave them an opportunity to offer a public thank-you to those who had helped them. (I am always deeply touched when I get a call, note, or e-mail from someone who has just finished the conversion process; it means a lot to me, and I suspect it does to others as well.)

Also, preparing for such a speech can lead to a review of the process, which can result not only in greater self-understanding but also, very importantly, in an increased understanding of conversion by the born-Jewish community.

I need to make a personal point here. I was raised in a secular-to-Reform Jewish household, but it was not so secular that I didn't learn that converts somehow were suspect, that they weren't genuine Jews, and that conversion was done by Christians, not Jews. My wife Sharon was raised in a Conservative-to-Orthodox Jewish household and she learned the same lessons about conversion. I have a feeling that a lot of born Jews carry this unfortunate legacy from childhood around with them. It is therefore an extremely valuable educational experience for born Jews to hear the story of a person's journey to Judaism. In addition, hearing how attached new Jews are to their religion can make born Jews come to appreciate the heritage they were born with (and may have taken for granted) in a new way.

Q. What is my romantic partner's role in conversion?

Epstein. Many people who are considering conversion to Judaism have a Jewish romantic partner. The reactions of those born

Jewish to their partners' choices varies greatly. Most born Jews are, of course, pleased. They provide constant support and help.

Some want it very much and raise the issue. A few use unfair emotional pressure. This pressure should be resisted. It is important to stress that a sincere conversion must be a person's own, undertaken without emotional blackmail or any other kind of pressure. The impetus for conversion must come from within. One convert, now a rabbi, expressed this in very blunt terms:

> If you are contemplating conversion for marriage, ask yourself how you will feel if your marriage later breaks up. For that matter, find out if your conversion will be a cause of marital discord, either because of your own ambivalence about the decision when faced with Christmas and Easter, or because your spouse chose you as a partner at least partly because you were *not* Jewish. Both of these are potential problems.
>
> Ask yourself how you are going to feel when confronted with major Christian holidays. Can you dump the Christmas tree? Can you contend with a born-Jewish spouse who *wants* a tree, without realizing that no former Christian can successfully divorce the tree from its religious symbolism?

Some born Jews very much want their partner to convert but are reluctant for various reasons to raise the option. Indeed, I am frequently surprised at how often a person who converts tells me that he or she would have done so years before but neither their Jewish partner nor anyone else raised the possibility. A favorite story that illustrates this came from a rabbi. This rabbi was speaking about how wonderful conversion is for the unity of the Jewish family, and he encouraged people to raise the issue with their Gentile partners. At that point, a woman in the audience rose to speak. She said she had been married for many years but had not raised the issue because she was certain that her husband would resist the whole idea of conversion. The rabbi paused and then asked if she were certain. She said that she was, but if the rabbi wanted some verification he could have it because he could ask her husband who was sitting next to her. The rabbi looked at the man and did ask. To his wife's surprise, the man said he had always found Judaism attractive but had not considered conversion because no one had ever asked him before.

Some born Jews are indifferent to the idea of conversion because Judaism does not mean a lot in their own lives; their lives are secular and they are reluctant to ask their partners to believe what they do not and practice rituals they themselves do not find meaningful. They would not want to convert to another religion, and so they are reluctant to raise the issue.

One phenomenon that many people have observed is that when a conversion is taking place, the born-Jewish romantic partner becomes suddenly much more interested in Judaism. A reacquaintance with Judaism as an adult—when Jewish memories frequently stopped at age 13 with a bar or bat mitzvah—is sometimes eye-opening. Many born Jews are amazed to discover how wonderful their heritage is; they were still seeing it through essentially a child's eye, and that memory was not always pleasant. A psychologist named Gloria told me the story of her romantic partner who had formally left Judaism. They attended a bar mitzvah and found the rabbi extremely interesting. Slowly at first they began to attend Jewish services. Eventually Gloria converted and her partner returned to Judaism.

The most crucial role for a born-Jewish partner is to support the conversion candidate. More than one conversion student has mentioned a spouse or partner disinterested in Judaism. They have a right to question their own act of converting if their partner does not even care about Judaism.

The best, most tangible, form of support that a Jewish romantic partner can show is to attend an Introduction to Judaism or conversion class with their partner. Sometimes, such attendance is even mandated, for rabbis know how crucial the experience is and how helpful it can be for the born-Jewish partner.

In an interesting way, the method a couple uses to discuss conversion is a symbol of their overall ability to communicate as a couple. They need to be able to discuss conversion issues openly, to express their true feelings without fear of being ridiculed and even if they realize those feelings are not fair. Of course, both during and after a conversion, the Jewish partner can be a teacher and guide. If the Jewish partner does not know a lot about Judaism, learning together can help cement the relationship.

It is important for born Jews to admit their own lack of knowledge about Judaism if they have that lack. One of my uncles was reluctant to enter a synagogue. He had a doctoral degree from Columbia, had studied philosophy at Harvard, and was in all respects extremely intelligent. The brilliance he could display in the world, however, contrasted badly with his ignorance in synagogue, which deeply embarrassed him and so he understandably chose to avoid feeling embarrassed simply by not going to Jewish religious events.

There are a lot of people like my uncle in the Jewish world. We all need to find strategies to let them know they are welcome, for those of them who, unlike my uncle, are married to Gentiles, will be more supportive if they are less ambivalent about their own attitudes toward Judaism.

Let me summarize some guidelines that I have developed for a couple in which one partner is Jewish and the other is considering conversion to Judaism.

1. When the couple sees that the relationship is getting serious, the option of conversion to Judaism should be raised. In general, the earlier this issue is raised the more useful because it helps define the entire relationship.
2. Such a discussion about conversion should lead to a more complete discussion about the role of Judaism in the life of the couple. It is extremely common for young people in love to expect that the romantic feeling they truly have will remain, will be the core of their identity, and will help them defend themselves against the rest of the world. In fact, of course, romantic feelings cool down. Ethnic and religious identities tend to emerge frequently after marriage, sometimes, for example, when a child is born, when a parent dies, or at a particular holiday. They suddenly realize that the eth-

nic identity they had once belittled now has far more importance to them than they ever expected.

3. The Jewish partner needs to make a determined effort to learn Judaism as well if Jewish knowledge is needed.
4. Look for support groups if they are available at a local synagogue, Jewish Community Center, or Jewish Family Service agency.

Q. I've got Jewish in-laws. Do they have any role to play in my conversion?

Epstein. While most converts find their Jewish in-laws to be a source of support, others do not. Jewish families, like all families, differ greatly.

It is important for conversion candidates to understand that born Jews were frequently brought up with incomplete and often inaccurate information about conversion to Judaism. For example, I was brought up to believe that converts could not ever genuinely be Jewish. I always recall this background when someone wonders about conversion. They have to work through their own education.

Ironically, converts can help educate Jewish parents.

Here is some information for Jewish parents who have a son or daughter dating, engaged to, or married to someone who has converted to Judaism or who may convert in the future.

At first, many Jewish parents are concerned about their son or daughter being romantically involved with someone who was not born Jewish. Some parents experience feelings of pain, guilt, anger, and helplessness.

It is important to remember that if your son or daughter is married to someone who has converted to Judaism, then there is no intermarriage. An intermarriage means a marriage between someone born Jewish and someone born non-Jewish who has not converted.

If your son or daughter's partner has not yet converted, remember that, through your kindness and help, the partner may consider conversion.

If you are dealing with one of these situations, consider the following suggestions:

• Learn all you can about the subject of conversion to Judaism. There are some suggested readings in this book. Talk to a Conservative rabbi and to those who have converted. Learning is important because it can dispel many myths about conversion.

Many Jews were brought up to believe, for example, that welcoming converts has been outside the Jewish tradition. Remember that Abraham and Sarah were not born Jewish and Ruth was the great-grandmother of King David. A sincere convert is genuinely Jewish. The real Jewish tradition is to accept and welcome converts.

At one time in Jewish history Jews were able to announce the availability of conversion very openly. We stopped at one point mostly because we were persecuted when so many people actually did convert. Untold numbers of people have chosen to become Jewish in our history.

Learning about conversion is important in order to accept and welcome converts. Such learning will increase knowledge about some of the reasons why converts will help the Jewish people:

1. Converts will add to our numbers.
2. Increased conversions among the romantically involved will reduce intermarriages.
3. Converts will make their own unique and special contributions to Jewish life.
4. Seeing someone want to become Jewish should make all born Jews reflect on the value of their heritage.

• Express and explore your feelings. Talk over your feelings with your son or daughter, other members of your family, and friends. Of course, talk to a rabbi and others who can provide professional advice and help. Most Jewish parents who have a new son-in-law or daughter-in-law who has converted become proud that the person has chosen to become Jewish.

Also, be sensitive to the needs of the person who has converted or is considering doing so. Obviously, such a time can include uncertainty and confusion. Also be sensitive to language. Some people who have become Jewish prefer to be called a "Jew by Choice," or a "Choosing Jew," or some other name. Some find the term "convert" offensive.

• If your son or daughter's partner has not converted, help the partner learn about conversion to Judaism. Very frequently in a relationship that could lead to or already is an intermarriage, no one in the family even suggests examining the option of conversion. Of course, do not use any kind of threat or pressure. Love, kindness, and patience are the keys here.

• If your son or daughter's partner is converting or has converted accept and welcome that partner. It is vital also to help the partner become part of Jewish life. This can be done by patiently answering questions, but don't worry if you don't know the answers. You can ask a rabbi and learn more about Judaism. Explain all you can about a Jewish home. It is especially important to give a new Jew a sense of feeling part of the Jewish people, of pride in being Jewish, and knowledge about some of the expressions, food, attitudes, and so on. Celebrate with that partner. Have a Sabbath meal together. Have a Passover seder. Observe all the holidays you do ordinarily, but do it together. If you don't celebrate many traditions yet, teaching a newcomer to Judaism about those traditions provides a good opportunity for you to celebrate more of them. Actually, when someone in a family converts it is common that all the born Jews in the family learn more about their own Jewish heritage as the convert learns. If appropriate, go to conversion ceremonies where you can. Give Jewish gifts. Your patience, humor, and support can bring the entire family closer together.

• Help your grandchildren lead Jewish lives. Stay in touch with them, taking care of them when you can. Tell them stories about your parents, about your own life, and about your son or daughter. With permission, give them Jewish books, music, videos, and other presents. It would be very helpful if you prepared a family tree so your grandchildren will know their roots. Write down or prepare an audiocassette or videotape in which you tell the stories that you remember over the years and want to pass on to your family.

• Let the Jewish community know how wonderful it is to welcome those who become Jewish. Letting people know of your positive experiences will help other Jewish parents with new Jews in their families.

Jewish life is always exciting. Part of the new Jewish world is the large number of people who have chosen to become Jewish. There are about 200,000 Jews by Choice in the United States today. These people need your support and your acceptance.

Q. Many born Jews emphasize their ethnicity, which is something I can never have. What should I do?

Epstein. You can't change the facts of your birth, but becoming Jewish means joining a people, not just accepting a religion. To join a people, you need to learn how those people act. By the way, many (but by no means all) U.S. Jews come from an Ashkenazic background. Ashkenazic (plural Ashkenazim) refers to Jews who can trace their ancestors to medieval Germany. Generally, the families traveled east to Poland and Russia. Most Jews in the United States had ancestors who came from these places, spoke Yiddish, and shared a way of life and common values. However, there are some Sephardic Jews in the United States as well. The Sephardi (Sephardim) are Jews who are descended from ancestors who lived in Spanish countries, such as Spain and Portugal. In Israel, there are many, many ethnic groups since Israel is a gathering place for Jews from literally all over the world. So there is an Israeli culture, which in many respects is different from the Ashkenazic culture of American Jews. Thus, Jews have many cultures.

My general advice to people becoming Jewish is to absorb the culture of the people among whom you live. In the United States that means particular efforts described in the next question.

The principal challenge is a change of consciousness. A new Jew must take on a new identity and, with it, new concerns in life. As someone newly Jewish, a convert must think and feel as a member of the Jewish community, identifying with the community's joys and sorrows. The Jewish community is concerned with the fate of Israel; so must the new Jew be. The Jewish community is concerned with anti-Semitism, with Jewish survival and continuity. This latter concern is shown by efforts in education, marriage to a Jewish partner, raising a Jewish family, and in other ways. This last point shows some difficulties. The convert must emphasize to his or her children the importance of marrying a Jewish partner. (Of course, someone who converts to Judaism prior to a marriage is Jewish.) The possible emotional tensions involved are very real.

There is no question that feeling Jewish will take time and concerted effort. The mark of success will be for those who have joined the Jewish people to feel as though their fate and the fate of their families is bound together with the fate of the Jewish people.

Q. How can I learn Jewish culture?

Epstein. Those who join the Jewish people not only have to learn the beliefs and practices of a new religion, but they must also become part of an ethnic group. Conversion to Judaism takes an extended time of adaptation precisely because so much needs to be absorbed. During the time of learning, many who become Jewish feel awkward or even still feel like outsiders despite the fact that they have converted. There are several steps to take to speed up the process of learning Jewish culture and feel a part of the Jewish group as well as the Jewish religion.

Here are some suggestions for developing a Jewish ethnic and cultural consciousness:

1. Learn some Hebrew and Yiddish non-religious terms that are commonly used. These, of course, should be in addition to Hebrew and other terms used for religious purposes. Leo Rosten's book *The Joys of Yiddish* (New York: McGraw-Hill, 1968) is particularly funny and useful. Other, more recent, books on Yiddish sayings are also useful. To get you started, here are a few commonly used Yiddish words:

a. *mensch* (rhymes with "bench"). A good, decent person. ("He's a real mensch.")
b. *schlepp* (rhymes with "pep"). To drag behind. ("Don't schlepp that all the way over here.")
c. *potchkeh* (rhymes with "notch ka"). A playful slap; to waste time. ("Don't potchkeh around, we've got work to do.")

2. Learn the names (and tastes) of some key foods. Include, among others, challah (braided bread), gefilte fish, tsimmes (a side dish of carrots and prunes), kreplach (dough filled with meat), and latkes (pancakes made of grated potatoes and fried in oil).

3. Listen to some Jewish comedians. There is a special brand of Jewish humor that is part of American Jewish ethnic identification. Of course, other aspects of culture (especially Jewish-oriented movies, music, and books) are also helpful.

These and similar activities can make new Jews become comfortable with their Jewish identity.

Q. How can I learn about Zionism and Israel?

Epstein. Israel is the center of contemporary Jewish life and the ancient home of the Jewish people. While Jews can disagree over the particular policies of an Israeli government, there is near unanimity in the Jewish view that Israel is vital to Jewish survival and central to Jewish existence. It is, therefore, extremely important that as a new Jew or someone thinking about joining the Jewish people, you come to understand the importance of Israel.

There are many wonderful books about Zionism, the modern movement to recreate the Jewish nation in the land of Israel, and about Israel itself. There are also wonderful films such as *Exodus* and numerous Israeli films. By far the best way to learn, though, is to travel to Israel. Travel is safe, and there is just no adequate substitute for feeling the land, talking with the people, and seeing all the famous sites including the Western Wall, the most sacred site in Judaism.

To begin learning, I would suggest following stories about Israel in the news. Subscribe to Jewish papers and magazines. Join pro-Israel organizations. Hadassah is one such wonderful organization that is aimed at women. There are many other groups. There are frequent lectures about Israel at synagogues and Jewish Community Centers.

A more subtle but equally important part of learning is to develop a natural feeling of protectiveness toward Israel, to identify with its need for security, its hunger for peace within that security, and its ultimate desire to be so good and so just a nation that it can serve as a model for all other nations.

II
AFTER THE CONVERSION

8

The Emotional Aspects
of Conversion

Q. What are the emotional aspects of conversion?

Epstein. Conversion to Judaism is a symbolic rebirth of the self. Such an awesome enterprise inevitably leads to frequently intense emotional reactions, from great joy and awe to deep moments of doubt and despair. It is important for a conversion candidate to be aware of some of the most common feelings. These include: (1) a sense of the loss of a previous identity, a feeling that I will discuss in the next question; (2) a sense of being overwhelmed; (3) a feeling of marginality; (4) confusion about dealing with previously celebrated holidays, especially Christmas and Easter; and (5) uncertainty about raising children as Jewish.

Leaving aside the first for a moment, let us consider the others.

It is common to feel overwhelmed. In part this involves accumulation of a great deal of knowledge. Joining a people and learning a new religion includes new ideas, customs, language, and much else. The sheer amount of what a person could know is, indeed, overwhelming. Even though many born Jews do not know an adequate amount about their own heritage, those who choose Judaism still frequently feel a moral obligation to learn all they can. This admirable feeling can also lead to a feeling of intellectual inadequacy. Hebrew, for example, is a big stumbling block for many people, including many extremely intelligent and successful people.

Beyond this, feelings of inadequacy can arise from feeling oneself not ready or good enough to become Jewish. I am surprised at how many people have expressed this feeling to me. They don't know if they are good enough. Maybe they have a handicap or are out of work. Maybe they are not white. Maybe they had an inadequate amount of schooling. Judaism, it should be repeated here, is open to all sincere converts. Learning for all Jews is a lifelong goal, not one that can be accomplished in six months or a year.

I think of a high school teacher of mine. Born in France, he struggled to learn English. Then one day, while thinking, he blurted out an idea. What surprised him was that he spoke English. Acquiring a Jewish identity is like that. You keep learning it and one day, probably without you being aware of the process, you will notice that you are thinking like a Jew.

Another element of feeling overwhelmed is the sense that a change of identity is so big that it is impossible to handle all its aspects; there is just too much to it. I don't think this feeling should be suppressed. It is important and should be listened to. Try normal relaxation techniques, keeping a journal, talking about your feelings with friends, rabbis, or others.

Some people leaving one identity and becoming Jewish feel a sense of marginality, that is, of being uncertain about their real religious identity, of being on the margin between their old and their new selves. This most frequently happens right after the conversion has been completed. The convert is now officially Jewish, having completed a period of study and all requirements. Yet, despite this accomplishment, the person does not yet feel fully Jewish and may not feel ready to let go of some religious aspects of a previous identity. In most cases, this common feeling simply is a matter of time. It takes time to accept the new Jewish identity, to live and breathe as a Jew.

If you feel this way, you may be able to speed up the process of feeling on the margin. Get involved in Jewish life. Definitely join a synagogue and go as often as you can. Perform Jewish tasks, such as studying or raising Jewish children. More than one parent (born Jewish as well) has learned a lot from studying with their children as the children attend religious classes.

Dealing with holidays can also be difficult. (I will discuss dealing with Christmas; see page 104.) Christian holidays have inherent tensions for born Christians who have converted to Judaism. Religious holidays have rituals that may evoke pleasantly nostalgic memories, since they are the family gathering days that punctuate the year. The most useful advice for converts is to emphasize family get-togethers on neutral holidays such as Thanksgiving or the Fourth of July.

It is also important not to be surprised at feelings of the past tugging at the present. Those feelings are real and should not be repressed. Instead, talk to peers who have gone through similar experiences.

Q. Will I feel my past identity has been lost when I convert?

Epstein. I have heard from several converts who, after their conversion to Judaism, had trouble letting go of their previous religious identity. Some hid away in a drawer religious symbols of their childhood. Others just felt confused or unhappy. Of course, each case is different. It is useful to discuss concerns with a rabbi or, if serious, even a professional counselor.

I think one key way to approach the problem is to take seriously the notion of Judaism as being a rebirth. If we keep that image, then the previous self "died" in a symbolic way. The new Jewish self is still mourning the "death." One possible approach is to consider this and undergo a formal mourning process for the previous self. Remember, though, that if this is more serious than a simple struggle, then do not necessarily take this advice, but meet with a licensed therapist.

Q. How can I feel Jewish?

Epstein. I have tried to sum this up in various places, but, in general, it is important to feel Jewish. I have these specific words of advice based on hearing from many converts: (1) read a lot of Jewish material. You are looking for intellectual models, people who think in a Jewish way. At first you may be imitating others, but as you learn more about the various issues of Jewish life, you will formulate your own ideas; (2) meet a lot of Jews. Join a synagogue, a Jewish Community Center, a Jewish organization. Get involved; (3) give yourself some time. A Jewish identity isn't built in a day.

Q. What should the Holocaust mean to me as a convert?

Epstein. I was once writing an article about a teacher whose subject was the Holocaust. For the article, I was interviewing students in the teacher's class. One of the students told me she had nightmares about the Holocaust; it felt sometimes as though time had disappeared and she was in Poland in the 1940s. The woman who told me the story was raised as a Christian and was born after the Holocaust ended. Her family did not come from Poland, and she lost no direct relatives in the Holocaust.

What had happened was that her Jewish identity had become so strong that she could feel like a Jew.

The experience of the Holocaust, indeed of anti-Semitism in general, should be a source of memory and education but not of fear.

The Holocaust was a shaping event in Jewish history in the twentieth century. *Yom Hashoah*, the holy day devoted to remembering the Holocaust, is the most recent holy day added to the Jewish calendar. It is important to remember, to read, to listen to Holocaust survivors, to know the dangers that the Jewish community has faced.

I've spoken with children of Nazis who converted to Judaism in order to atone. I've spoken to Christians who felt they were replacing one of the million and a half Jewish children who perished during the Holocaust. Clearly, as an event, the Holocaust has had a searing power on the conscience of decent people, and a powerful reminder to Jews that they have potentially deadly enemies. The lesson that many Jews have drawn from the Holocaust, the lesson summed up in the oft-quoted expression "Never Again," is that Jews must, after the Holocaust, remain ever-vigilant to hatred and must resist evil quickly when they encounter it.

Q. What should my relationship to Israel be?

Epstein. As I suggested earlier (page 87), no single event in the last 1,900 years has been as positive for the Jewish community as the rebirth of Israel in 1948. As a new Jew, Israel is your second home, a place to visit. Indeed, for some, it is a place to live. Your relationship needs to be close. Of course, you need not agree with every policy of an Israeli government to support it.

The best single step is to visit. In any case, plan to send your children for a visit. It was an extraordinarily moving moment in my family's history when my daughter Elana had a Bat Mitzvah in the oldest synagogue in the world on Masada, the sheared-off plain in the Judean desert where Jews once defended themselves against the Roman conquerors and chose death over a life as slaves. Today, Masada is a symbol of determination to live. With my wife and all four children standing there, looking over the vast sands, it became impossible not to feel deeply a part of the land and the people.

It is also important to support Israel. Perhaps plant a tree or donate to some worthy Israeli institution, or buy Israel Bonds. All are important so that you feel a personal stake in Israel's survival and well-being. The more you feel that Israel is truly a Jewish homeland destined to be a light unto the nations, as Isaiah proclaimed, the more you will feel the needed connection and sense of responsibility for Israel.

Q. Are there support groups for converts?

Epstein. Check with your local synagogue, Jewish Community Center, and Jewish family service agency for any existing support groups. If none exist, consider starting one of your own. Better yet, help your congregation start a *keruv* committee that includes a support group.

One significant contribution congregations can make to attract, train, and welcome converts to Judaism is to have a *keruv*, or outreach committee. *Keruv* is a Hebrew word meaning to "draw in." *Keruv* seeks to draw interested people to Judaism without changing Jewish standards. *Keruv* is used here instead of the word "outreach" because reaching out may be interpreted as modifying Judaism in order to attract outsiders, whereas *keruv* clearly means that Judaism remains the same as it welcomes those who wish to join it. Obviously individual committees can choose the name that they believe best suits them. For the purposes of this material, the terms are interchangeable.

Keruv, or outreach, is meant not only for unconverted gentile partners in an intermarriage, but also for others, such as those who have already converted, and for all those with a spiritual interest in Judaism. Interestingly, many born Jews benefit greatly from *keruv* because, as they welcome non-Jews, they learn more about their own Judaism.

A congregational *keruv* committee can have several purposes. It can: (1) be a support group for converts; (2) help to integrate new converts into the congregational community; (3) serve as a source of information about conversion to Judaism for those in the congregation who are intermarried and are not Jewish; and (4) develop educational programs about Judaism and conversion for the congregation and the wider community. There are, of course, many other possible purposes.

A *keruv* committee needs someone to initiate it, either a rabbi, a congregational leader, or a congregant. That person needs to meet with the rabbi and other interested people. The rabbi's support is, of course, vital.

If you wish to organize such a committee at your congregation, talk with all the leaders of the congregation to seek ideas and approval. Then simply ask various people about who might be interested in such a committee. Use word-of-mouth to find five or six people. Call these people and ask if they would be interested in attending a meeting with the rabbi and other needed people.

The first meeting is important. It is vital to determine the specific purpose and structure of the group. Of course, a group can have several interrelated purposes. It is useful to have either one leader or a rotating leadership. It is also important to determine the eligibility for membership in the group. For example, you might decide that your group will be open to converts, their spouses, born Jews interested in the subjects, and even anyone outside the congregation who wishes to learn about conversion or discuss it. (Obviously, this is a way ultimately to attract new members.)

A *keruv* committee can undertake a variety of projects depending on the interests and goals of the group. Many activities can be free or low cost, that is, *keruv* need not take monies from other vital programs within the synagogue. It is also a good idea to start with only one project, carry it through, evaluate it, and learn from it.

It is also crucial that a *keruv* committee's members be clear in their own feelings about the importance of conversion and express this view publicly when they discuss *keruv*.

There are many possible activities for a *keruv* group. Here are some of them:

1. Simply meet and discuss the experiences, joys, and difficulties of conversion, such as relations with parents, children, and the born Jewish community. Telling and hearing stories is helpful and fascinating.
2. Discuss those experiences in a public forum. You can send out news releases to newspapers and cable tv stations, which may print and broadcast notice of the meeting for free. You can also decide to place advertisements in a local newspaper.

3. Have lectures by a group member with a special story, or bring in an outside lecturer on the subject.
4. Establish a *keruv* center in the library, with books and articles on the subject. If your synagogue sells books, have some titles on conversion available.
5. Meet with the synagogue staff regarding responding to questions about conversion.
6. Write articles about the group for the synagogue bulletin.
7. Support or establish an Introduction to Judaism program aimed at Gentiles who wish to learn about Judaism and explore the possibility of conversion.
8. Establish a host family program for new converts. In such a program, synagogue members show new Jews how to live Jewishly. Some areas of help might be in prayer, keeping a kosher home, keeping Shabbat, cooking, preparing a seder, and so on.
9. Work within the congregation to provide congregational members with reliable information about conversion. Ask the rabbi to include discussion of conversion in a sermon. Plan and hold public conversion ceremonies for those who wish it. Meet with students in the congregational school to discuss conversion and answer questions about it. Ask congregational men's and women's organizations to hold meetings on the subject.
10. Develop a package of materials for Gentiles who ask about conversion to Judaism.

Keruv committees in each congregation would enrich and strengthen Jewish life.

9

After the Conversion . . .
Some Questions

Q. How can I honor my gentile parents? I'm really worried about what to do when they die. Can I say Kaddish?

Epstein. The heart of your attitude toward parents comes, of course, from the Fifth Commandment, to honor your parents. It is important to maintain a close relationship with them, but also vital to draw needed lines. They should respect your religious choices and the way you raise your children. In particular, it is often suggested that Jewish children should not be exposed to the specifically religious ceremonies of the Gentile family.

If a parent gets sick, that parent should be visited in accordance with the *mitzvah* ('religious commandment') of *bikur cholim* ('Visiting the Sick'). Different rabbis have different positions about attending non-Jewish religious services, so it is best to check with the rabbi at your synagogue or a local rabbi if you do not belong to a synagogue.

Most rabbis I have spoken with (though not all) strongly recommend that a convert observe Jewish mourning rituals for Gentile parents. This includes sitting shiva (observing a mourning period for seven days after the day of burial, which is considered the first day) and saying Kaddish, a prayer for the dead.

Q. Will I always feel like a convert?

Epstein. No. You'll feel like what you are—someone who is Jewish. The acceptance of a new identity naturally takes time.

Although many people disagree with me, I think it is healthy for converts to retain some aspect of a conversionary identity. They are able to provide unique and fascinating advice and information for born Jews. They can counsel and support others who wish to join the Jewish people. Finally, by being open about conversion, they remove any sense of shame or self-doubt some may feel by making it a source of celebration. I hear from people who have converted years ago and still feel that is an important part of them. Their conversionary status doesn't make them less of a Jew. In my eyes at least, it adds a special flavor to their Jewishness.

Q. Can I ever return to my previous religion?

Epstein. In general, most rabbis I have spoken with affirm that when a person is born Jewish or converts to Judaism, that person remains a Jew forever. However, some people—born Jews as well as converts—may abandon Judaism and attach themselves to another religion. They are technically apostates who remain Jews and who must atone for their sins if they wish to return formally, although they remain Jews.

The abandonment of Judaism means the loss of certain privileges of a Jewish identity although not the loss of a total Jewish identity. For example, the supreme court in Israel has ruled that those born or converted Jews who join a Gentile religious movement have lost the privileges granted Jews under the Law of Return in Israel; this right guarantees Jews automatic citizenship in Israel.

Interestingly, most rabbis also say that if a woman leaves Judaism, any children she has subsequently are legally Jewish.

Q. Will born Jews always think of me as a convert?

Epstein. I don't think so, although in the near future a substantial minority probably will. The reason for this is a long-standing negative Jewish attitude toward converts. (See Chapter 11 for an expanded explanation of the origins of the negative views of converts and the reasons Jews should not hold those attitudes.)

I was raised with such an attitude as a child. When the rabbi of my local congregation married a convert, the people in the congregation were deeply confused. I was only about 12 years old at the time and do not remember much about it other than the gossip and negative feelings. I know from talking with many born Jews that they, too, were raised with these attitudes. Changing such a long-standing belief will take time, but this effort can be accelerated by converts speaking out and telling their stories; this gives conversion a human face.

10
Children and Conversion

Q. Can my minor children whom I converted change their minds when they grow up if they don't want to be Jewish?

Epstein. As previously discussed, a minor child converted by his or her parents is considered fully Jewish even without the child being able to consent to the conversion. Such a converted infant can officially renounce the conversion at the age Jews consider maturity: 13 for a male and 12 for a female. Lacking a specific desire to give up the Jewish identity, the converted person is then Jewish for life as described above.

Q. What do I tell my children about my conversion?

Epstein. It is, of course, important to tell your children the truth about your conversion. In general, I am in favor of telling children as early as possible, certainly long before they might hear it from a family member, friend, or classmate. For a young child, there is an excellent children's book that can serve as a model. This is

Mommy Never Went to Hebrew School by Mindy Avra Portnoy (Rockville, MD: Kar-Ben Copies, 1989).

What is crucial in talking with children is to tell them that they are Jewish, not of mixed religions. Reducing any mixed signals is vital for children to establish clear and unambiguous religious identities.

Q. What should I do about Christmas?

Epstein. A common problem for all Jews in an overwhelmingly Christian society like the United States is dealing with even relatively benign holidays in which Christian identity is expressed. The most obvious case is that of Christmas. Many Jewish families face this "December dilemma" during which Hanukkah, a minor religious Jewish holiday, has become a very important Jewish holiday in the United States because it is one way Jews have to "compete" with Christmas.

For the convert, Christmas contains all these emotional tensions and many others. It is common, for instance, for converts to recall fond Christmas memories, childhood moments of unwrapping presents under a tree and so on. Some born Jews and converts keep a tree, but most, knowing this is outside the Jewish tradition, do not. I strongly believe it is confusing especially for children to keep a tree in a Jewish home. Also, converts deal with their families, often in a religious context.

Christmas, then, can be a struggle. Other holidays can be as well. Children may want to color eggs at Easter; converts may recall Easter meals, church experiences, Easter egg hunts and so on. It is important not to repress the memories. They helped form the person.

It is very valuable to discuss these issues in a support group and to fill Christian holidays with Jewish counter-programming, using the days to read Jewish books and have Jewish experiences.

Q. How can I help educate my children?

Epstein. Some converts have told me of their feelings of inadequacy toward raising Jewish children because they were not brought up in a Jewish home. It is crucial if you have this feeling to make sure your Jewish identity is strong and to identify the sort of Jewish identity you want your children to have. What kind of education will bring about that identity? What kind of experiences? What can you do to structure the home environment to enhance that identity? Maybe, for example, you'll choose to have a Sabbath meal each Friday night.

Then put all these ideas into practice. Add a Jewish part to all you do. In a picture album for a child, add the child at Jewish events. If at all possible, take children to Jewish sites, such as a Jewish museum or, best of all, Israel.

As all parents know, it is valuable to learn with your children. Make sure your children receive a Jewish education. Study with them. Go over their homework from religious school. Ask them to teach you; they will learn the material very well if they pretend to be a teacher.

Join a synagogue, Jewish Community Center, and Jewish organizations. Read Jewish books. Watch Jewish films. Subscribe to Jewish periodicals.

With all this, your children will become educated Jews secure and happy in their identity.

Q. How can I tell my children to marry someone Jewish when I'm a convert?

Epstein. You're not a convert; you're Jewish, and as a Jewish parent proud of a Jewish identity, concerned about the Jewish future, and desirous of having Jewish grandchildren, you can and should advise your children to marry someone who is Jewish.

You can do this without denigrating people from other backgrounds, without showing any disrespect for other spiritual traditions, and without belittling people with different beliefs. Indeed, your choosing Judaism when you didn't have to underscores your ability to understand the incredible value of a Jewish heritage. It is this sense of heritage you need to communicate.

Let me now turn to a subject vital to the Jewish community. This question raises the whole issue of intermarriage.

Because I write a lot about intermarriage and conversion to Judaism, I frequently get asked questions related to these subjects. Although I'm not a rabbi, a psychologist, or a professional counselor, I try my best to answer based on what I've seen. Recently, the most common question has been from anguished, committed Jewish parents—Jews by birth as well as Jews by choice—who are unsure what to say to their son or daughter who is interdating a kind and nice Gentile.

Because such questions emerge at a time of emotional stress, it is not a good time to raise issues that can and should be raised with Jewish parents of young children. Those are the issues of prevention, that is, how can interdating and intermarriage be prevented before they occur. It is crucial for parents of younger Jews to stress Jewish education, formal Jewish activities, such as joining and attending synagogues and practicing Jewish rituals in the home, and informal Jewish activities such as visiting Israel or attending Jewish camp, and to discuss issues of interdating before it occurs precisely to remove the emotion from the subject. One important issue, for instance, is the stereotyping of Jews by other Jews. The most prominent of such stereotyping, perhaps, is for Jewish males to see Jewish females, that is, potential dates and marriage partners, as "Jewish American Princesses," and thus unpleasant prospects for dating or marriage. Jewish parents and educators must work persistently to confront and break down such stereotypes.

It is also important for Jewish parents to be able to articulate why they want their children to marry other Jews. Many of those young people announce their engagement only to be shocked at the depth of concern seemingly suddenly shown by their Jewish parents.

Jewish parents will have different reasons for wanting to have their children avoid intermarriage. Some parents, for instance, will focus on the importance of Jewish survival, or on marrying someone Jewish as being a *mitzvah*, a religious obligation, or on the mission that the Jewish people have, or on maintaining the Jewish culture, or on any of a variety of other reasons. Whatever those reasons, it is important in general for rabbis, Jewish communal leaders, and Jewish parents to define and explain them before interdating starts.

When such preventative techniques haven't been applied or haven't been effective (they are, after all competing in crucial respects against American popular culture, the lure of romance, and the undeniable power of hormonal and other forms of attraction), and a Jewish son or daughter is interdating, it becomes time for troubled Jewish parents to discuss that specific issue.

There obviously is no single or best answer for these Jewish parents, in large part because the age at which such interdating occurs differs so much, as do the seriousness of that dating, the interpersonal relationships between the parents and son or daughter, and other crucial factors.

Nevertheless, there are some guidelines for Jewish parents that might be useful and adaptable to individual situations. Parents should not be shocked by outrageous comments. Sons and daughters love to test their parents' limits of patience and sometimes float ideas just to gauge the reactions of their parents and see the limits the parents impose. Additionally, Jewish parents should speak about what interdating means for the son or daughter as individuals, not necessarily what interdating means to the Jewish people, unless the son or daughter is old enough to understand and identify with such issues.

One way to begin is simply to raise the issue, to cite your concern. Again depending on the nature of the relationship, a Jewish parent might say something like, "I know you and _____ are dating, and I wanted to discuss that with you. I want you to understand my concerns for you and your future, especially if you get serious with someone who is not Jewish."

Many young people at this point may feel or say, "It's my life," or "It's none of your business," or "It's not up to you. It's up to me." Many Jewish children are raised to talk back to authority, to question, so it is not surprising that they will question either their parents or their parents' values. Many Jewish parents feel awkward in raising the issue itself, because their self-definition is often one of being tolerant people, yet here they are arguing against tolerating a non-Jewish partner for their son or daughter. That is why parents need to understand themselves and their own views before they speak to their children.

Such a talk need not challenge a son or daughter's call to privacy. A parent might compare the situation to a friend trying to help a friend. Saying something like "You're right, but because we care for you so much and don't want to see you hurt, we'd like to discuss this with you. If a good friend thought you might be doing something that could hurt you, that friend would want to say something. So do we."

One approach I take with some teenagers is to ask them to remember their lives 10 (or some number) years before. Therefore, if they are now 18 I ask them to recall being 8 years old. I then ask them if they would have liked decisions they made at age 8 to affect them now at 18. They are always quite sure that they would not like this. I then tell them that they will change as much between 18 and 28 as between 8 and 18 and they should be careful, because the choices they make now will affect them and when they get to age 28 they may not be so happy about some of the choices.

Both teenagers and older Jews will sometimes raise the question of prejudice, accusing the Jewish parent of being discriminatory or even racist: "Are Jews the only good people?" The answer to such an approach is not, of course, to argue that Jews are better. Young people know that there are good Gentiles and some not-so-good Jews. The approach I often take is to ask young Jews: "Would you go out with absolutely anyone who asked you?" When they say no, I say, "Then are you being prejudiced against those you don't go out with? No. It's not prejudice. You're just using your judgment; you're using certain criteria to decide who to date. If those criteria are based on who would be a good date for you, then they're not prejudicial. One of those criteria should be that the person is Jewish because he or she is likely to share your values and background. You'll know what to expect from them on a date, and they'll know what to expect from you." For older Jews, it is possible to discuss the distinctive values of Judaism that can be passed on, or, with young Jews who don't know those distinctive values, to help them learn more about Judaism.

Again, depending on age, there are different questions to raise and different problems to solve. Should the 15-year-old date a Gentile? Should a 19-year-old away at college date a Gentile? Should a 22-year-old college graduate date a Gentile? It doesn't make much sense to talk about marriage to the 15-year-old, whereas the 22-year-old, who is certainly of marriageable age, should discuss such a possibility.

The purely dating—unrelated to marriage—question is complex because parents want children to be popular and to date. I believe, though, that a dating pattern develops early, as does what might be called a mate-appropriateness debate between parents and child that will emerge later. Put simply, encouraging and accepting "innocent" dates between Jews and Gentiles early on establishes the acceptability of such a practice and makes it harder to argue against later. Mature parents know more than immature teens; the parents know there will be many people to date. If there are few potential dates and if they are deemed unacceptable, the option for Jewish parents is not to accept interdating but to find ways to expand the potential dating circle for their children. This can be done by working with local Jewish congregations and community centers to expand Jewish singles groups, such as organizing singles groups on a regional rather than on a strictly local basis. Of course, the density of the Jewish population is an important factor. Joining a large congregation; enrolling a student in a school with a large Jewish population; living, if possible, in a location with a large Jewish population; using Jewish population as a principal criterion for selecting a college—all these will add to the dating potential for young Jews. Additionally, parents in congregations or organizations should join together to form support groups to discuss these issues. If local Jewish congregations or community centers don't yet offer such groups, parents should ask that they be started or start one themselves. I've seen groups in which just parents and both parents and young people participated, and, even when there was no seeming solution, both parents and their children found the groups to be satisfying.

Young Jews will sometimes say and mean, "I'm not going to marry him. It's only a date." I try to look for a metaphor they will understand in explaining the notion of dating habits. For example, I have discussed learning to drive, an interest many young people have. A parent wouldn't want a young driver to practice for their driving test by driving on the wrong side of the road. Sure, it might be just practice and not a real driver's test, but learning correctly from the first will help when the real test comes along. Similarly, learning appropriate dating rights and wrongs from the beginning will help when it comes to selecting a marriage partner.

For older Jews who are of marriageable age, the discussion has to be more frank and more serious. Parents need to discuss with their older sons and daughters such subjects as the intimate relationship between interdating and intermarriage, the high failure rates of marriages in general and intermarriages in particular, the effects of assimilation on the future of the Jewish people, and the genuine feelings the young Jew has toward Jewishness.

One admittedly provocative approach here is for the Jewish parents simply to ask their son or daughter how he or she would feel if the Gentile partner wanted to baptize the child (or engage in other religious rites if the person being dated is not Christian), or if that Gentile's parent gave a child a cross for a present and so on. Deliberately suggestive images can be used in order to make the young Jew confront his or her own Jewish identity. A less provocative, though similar, approach is to play a word association game with both partners. Ask them each to tell what associations they have with particular words like "Jewish," "Christian," "Christmas," "family," and "children," and let them listen to each other.

Obviously, a more sophisticated approach is to have each explain their religious feelings to each other.

It is also difficult for a Jewish parent to puncture the powerful illusion that love conquers all. Having the couple themselves discuss religious issues may be the most revealing approach. Whatever the approach, it is vital for a parent or a rabbi or a counselor to raise these issues prior to an engagement.

Whatever is said, it is important for Jewish parents to convey their feelings honestly. If a potential marriage is pending, Jewish parents need to say, honestly, whether or not they will attend the wedding, how they will feel about the grandchildren, and so on. Such an honest talk unfortunately sometimes becomes a yelling match. Some parents, dramatically and at cross-purpose to their goals, hear of a potential intermarriage and simply scream. Many try guilt. Some talk about the many Jewish ancestors who make sacrifices for Judaism and who would be unbearably shocked to see one of their descendants intermarrying. Other parents passionately argue that by intermarrying their son or daughter is handing Hitler a posthumous victory by contributing to the destruction of the Jewish people, or, as has been done, they ask, "Who is your model, Anne Frank or Hitler?"

Honest Jewish parents, those who try to confront the problem openly and honestly, face a dilemma. Arguing against interdating shouldn't devolve into an argument that their son or daughter should have no Gentile friends, and yet, saying that, it sometimes becomes difficult to draw the line between friendship and romantic attachment. This is one of the real burdens of living in an open society. It is compounded by fluid dating styles in which dating has become much more informal than when today's Jewish parents were growing up and dating. However difficult the line might be to draw between friend and acceptable dating partner, it is real and young people have to learn it. Therefore, even if the person is "a nice girl" or "a good boy," it is important to say that being nice, and kind, and good are necessary ingredients for a good marriage partner, but they are not sufficient reasons. In addition to those qualities, the potential partner needs to be Jewish.

Some marriage-age Jews ask, "Wouldn't you rather I marry a kind Gentile I love than a Jew I hate?" What cruel-hearted parent would answer such a question by arguing for the marriage to the Jew? Of course, it is up to the parent to point out that the young Jew has committed the logical fallacy known as the law of the excluded middle. What Jewish parents want is for their son or daughter to marry a Jewish partner the son or daughter loves. Marrying an un-loved Jewish partner is not the single alternative to interdating or intermarriage. Further Jewish dating is the appropriate suggestion.

Finally, it is important to discuss conversion to Judaism. Here you can use your own example. This, of course, is especially true if the dating is serious or if an engagement or intermarriage has taken place. Again, conversion to Judaism is an important subject in Jewish history and not at all always intimately linked with in-termarriage. It is important for young Jews, especially those who are intermarried, to know that conversion to Judaism has a long and noble history within Judaism. For younger Jews especially, it is important to point out that the availability of conversion should not encourage and does not provide permission to intermarry. The reasons for this are that only about 5 percent of Gentiles who marry Jews convert, and even if a conversion occurs the Jewish child will confront loving Gentile grandparents who can, with the best of intentions, introduce non-Jewish elements into their lives.

Still, conversion remains an acceptable option. If the conver-sion occurs prior to what would have been an intermarriage, then no intermarriage occurs. Therefore, wider Jewish knowledge about conversion and acceptance of converts to Judaism may in fact dra-matically reduce the number of intermarriages. Introducing the idea of conversion to Judaism to the Gentile partner, indeed to other intermarried Gentiles as well, is a useful alternative to the guilt and despair some Jewish parents feel when their son or daughter intermarries.

Indeed, Jewish parents need to think carefully about what their reaction would be if an intermarriage does occur. That's too broad a subject to be covered in the response to this question, but in general it seems clear to me that the best approach is to maintain a close and loving relationship with the couple and their children, to reach out to them, to invite them to share the joys of an extended Jewish family life. Many young Jews discover the values of Judaism only after intermarrying. Many of their partners consider conversion only after marriage or the birth of children, who need caring and loving Jewish parents around to embrace them.

Jewish parents are residing in a new world of dating and marriage patterns. It is not an easy world to get used to inhabiting. Because of that, it is all the more important to raise these issues, to speak with each other openly about them, even to disagree, to accumulate suggestions, and weed out destructive tactics. At the very least, parents and children will talk with each other about issues that affect them the most profoundly.

III
IMPLICATIONS OF CONVERSION

11
The Born-Jewish Reaction
to Converts

Q. Why should Jews welcome converts?

Epstein. This is one of the most important questions in this book. Because of my own background of being taught that converts weren't genuinely Jewish and welcoming converts was not a legitimate activity for Jews, I want to talk at length about my own interest. Then I want to go on to discuss why Jews should welcome converts. This will include a discussion of what I believe to be a religious obligation to welcome converts, how welcoming converts helps Jewish continuity, and how welcoming converts can, in particular, help American Jews get a new purpose. I also want to look at arguments against welcoming converts and try to refute them all, and I, finally, wish to look at genuine problems for the Jewish community as it welcome converts in large numbers for the first time in almost 2,000 years.

All of these will be extended individual sections because I believe the general question of welcoming converts is at the heart of Jewish life.

Let me start, then, with my own background and how I developed an interest in the subject of conversion to Judaism.

I didn't grow up in a very religious home, but it was Jewish enough so that my parents made it clear that converts to Judaism were, in some fundamental way, not really Jewish. The occasion for this discussion was the marriage of our rabbi to a tall, blonde convert secretively referred to as "the shikse." I was 12 at the time and still recall the shocked whispers and excited gossip.

As I grew, I became interested in Judaism. I didn't much think about issues of conversion. They weren't very important to anyone I knew.

My next encounter with conversion came as I began to learn about contemporary Jewish life. I had read about the low Jewish birth rates, the aged population, the assimilation. I became concerned about how Jews could maintain their community. As I cast about for answers, I at first focused on how important it was to increase births. Then I read an article, "The Advisability of Seeking Converts," (Vol. 24, no. 1. Winter 1975: 49-57) in *Judaism* by Rabbi Gilbert Kollin, discussing the importance of seeking converts. I had never read an article on the subject, but this one made a good deal of sense.

In addition to increasing numbers of converts to Judaism, conversion, I soon discovered, was a Jewish response to what would be a central Jewish communal concern: the rise in intermarriage. In those heady days of the late 1970s and early 1980s it looked as though conversions prior to what would have been an intermarriage and, almost as frequently, after the marriage were actually adding to the Jewish population. I imagined some social scientist with a wicked sense of humor suggesting all Jews marry born Gentiles who would convert so we could increase our numbers. Although the boom in conversions soon busted, the subject had become central to Jewish life, especially after Rabbi Alexander Schindler, the influential president of the Union of American Hebrew Congregations (the Reform movement's central congregational body) gave an address in 1978 arguing that there be an attempt to interest the "unchurched" in becoming Jewish, especially those religiously unaffiliated people who were married to Jews.

Seeking converts to increase numbers and to prevent or alter an intermarriage were, of course, vital prudential reasons to offer Judaism. As arguments, they probably would have been sufficient to keep me interested in the efforts to welcome converts, as evidenced by the fact that I include them in the reasons given to be welcoming.

Then one day, I was reading an essay by David Ben-Gurion about Zionism. The essay was remarkable because Ben-Gurion spoke about the Jewish people's historic mission in redeeming humanity. Who knows how mental connections are made, but in that second I attached my growing interest in conversion to Ben-Gurion's comments. That is, I realized that there was more to conversion than the practical reasons. I thought seeking converts could somehow be intimately tied to a wider Jewish purpose than questions of demography and assimilation.

I then began to read sacred Jewish literature more systematically to understand if my intuition was borne out in Jewish thought. I was amazed at the centrality within Jewish philosophy of seeking converts to Judaism and its importance and eventual decline in Jewish life.

This extensive reading led me to an unusual conclusion: the Jewish people had a religious obligation to offer their religion to others and to welcome those who freely chose to become Jewish. That is, seeking converts became more than a useful antidote to social problems. I began to see it as a vital Jewish religious obligation. Actually, the useful and correct religious word to use here is "mission." The word had always had Christian overtones to me, but I now think that it is a useful word for what the Jews felt and did. This mission to seek converts was, at one time, understood and practiced, but it was a mission that until recently had been sadly neglected in Jewish life.

Let me explain why I think Jews have a religious obligation to welcome converts. It was once considered a Jewish religious obligation to welcome converts to Judaism, and it is vital that we reclaim that obligation. This welcoming attitude can be seen in sacred literature and Jewish history. That attitude changed over the course of Jewish history, and it is important to note the reasons for those changes in the Jewish view of the conversionary obligation. Those reasons will explain the inaccurate view that welcoming converts is somehow antithetical to traditional Judaism and provide a justification for a resumption of an ancient Jewish covenantal obligation.

The idea of the obligation to welcome converts starts with the concept of the Jewish people, divinely chosen, freely accepting an agreement with God. Part of that covenant was the Jewish task to bring God's universal moral message to all humanity by offering their faith, and to welcome converts who accept the particularities and obligations of the moral message.

The Jewish people saw such an obligation as stemming from a variety of sources, as principally seen in:

1. *God's actions:* God's revelation at Mount Sinai can be seen as the original model of an active offering of Judaism. By giving the Jewish people the Torah, God is sharing a faith.

2. *The actions of the founders and leaders of the Jewish people:* Abraham's gathering of "souls" in Haran (Genesis 12:5) was understood by the rabbis to mean that Abraham had gotten converts (e.g., Genesis Rabbah 39:21). Rabbi Hoshaya believed that Isaac sought converts, and Genesis 35:2 is understood in Genesis Rabbah as indicating that Jacob also sought converts. There is a wonderful passage in Exodus Rabbah (1:29) in which Moses confronts the Egyptian taskmaster beating the Hebrew slave. Moses foresees that there would not be a single convert from among the taskmaster's posterity; this perception allows Moses to proceed with killing the taskmaster.

Many prophets discussed conversion. In Jonah's physical voyage, we learn that God cares about the salvation of all people. Jeremiah was appointed a prophet to all the nations (Jeremiah 1:5), not just Israel. Isaiah, of course, talks about the Jewish people being "a light unto the nations" (Isaiah 42:6).

Ruth is probably the most famous convert in the Bible, in part because, as David's great-grandmother, she is the ancestor of the Messiah. The fact that the Book of Ruth is read on Shavuot shows that each time the Jewish people welcomes a convert it is as though we accept the Torah again.

All Jewish children are taught that Hillel could be quite brilliant, even while standing on one foot. We are not taught, however, that the mocking pagan who asked Hillel to explain the Torah in a single sentence was a would-be convert. Hillel was conducting a conversion class. Indeed, after explaining Judaism, Hillel told the man that study of the commentary was essential. The man did decide to become Jewish.

The most famous of the Talmudic passages specifically praising conversionary work is by the historically important Rabbi Elezar ben Pedat in Pesahim 87b, a passage in which it is asserted that God exiled Jews from their homeland for only one reason, to increase the number of converts. It is striking that so horrible an event as exile should be seen to have a divine use. That use, to seek converts, had to have been considered so valuable that it justified exile.

Much additional Jewish literature, from Midrashim to the Responsa of the Tosafists, speaks very favorably about Jews welcoming converts. For example, Va-Yikra Rabbah (6:5) says: "If you will not proclaim Me as God unto the heathen nations of the world, I shall exact penalty from you."

3. *The historical actions taken by the Jewish people:* Did the Jewish people actively seek converts? In part the answer to this question depends on the definition of "seeking." Jews did not, with rare exceptions, forcibly convert others or even publicly intrude on them, such as by standing on corners preaching Judaism. This was so in part because the prophetic vision was that one day all peoples would recognize the Lord. It was understood that not all people would, however, willingly accept all the obligations that Jews had. Therefore, the preaching was to all and the welcoming to those Gentiles who willingly wished to accept more than the seven commandments given as the Noahide laws and as obligatory for all humanity.

Jews engaged in what might be called "active welcoming." Such welcoming took several distinct forms. For example, Jews: (1) allowed and invited gentiles into the synagogues to see Jewish services; (2) created a variety of literature aimed at converts; (3) traveled widely and, as they went, responded to questions and explained Jewish beliefs and practices; (4) adopted Gentile children and raised them as Jews; and (5) effected the conversion of the Gentile partner in what would have been, or was, an intermarriage.

Judging by the demographic, literary, and archeological evidence, the Jews seemed to have been remarkably successful at winning converts and "sympathizers," that is, those people who practiced many Jewish customs, felt close to the Jews, but who didn't actually convert.

4. *Jewish law:* It is obvious that the very creation of Jewish law (*halachah*) concerning converts would not have arisen if converts were not welcome and did not choose to become Jewish. Why codify laws, that is, if Judaism didn't want or wasn't getting any converts? Indeed, the existence of the halachah is a form of offering. Crucially, the rules indicate that converts are permitted. Nowhere does the halachah forbid conversion and in fact, the halachic rules are there to show that Jews have thought about the question of conversion and considered it carefully. The existence of the rules of conversion in halachah gave Jews specific guidelines to show to potential converts; the Jews had a set series of rules and procedures that could be offered. The halachic procedure is described in a lengthy *baraita* (a statement not found in the Mishnah, the first authoritative compilation of oral law) in Yevamot 47 a,b. This procedure is, in effect, a guidebook for potential converts.

If this obligation can be seen in our sacred literature, and if we have historically engaged in active welcoming, and if we were successful, several questions remain. Why did our attitude toward conversion change and why did we stop actively welcoming converts? The divine obligation to welcome converts, once seen as a continuing symbol of accepting the Torah, gradually was transformed into an option, not an obligation, and was seen, ultimately, as distinctly un-Jewish. The reasons for this historic change are many, including:

1. Roman, Christian, and Muslim authorities persecuted the Jewish community for welcoming converts and persecuted the converts themselves. The anti-conversionary laws enacted endangered

the lives of Jews and would-be Jews. For instance, between 81 and 96 C.E. Domitian ordered that converts be put to death or sent into exile and their property seized. In 325 Constantine forbade the Jewish community from engaging in any proselytizing activities. While welcoming still occurred, over time the extent and severity of the laws made vulnerable Jewish communities much more reluctant to be active in welcoming converts. Communal survival began to challenge religious obligation. If welcoming converts was seen as a divine obligation, then such welcoming had to occur despite persecution. But if the welcoming was not seen as a divine obligation, but simply as a communal policy, then it could be abandoned in the face of persecution. This observation led Jews concerned about communal survival to search for a religious justification not to welcome converts actively.

2. Christians and later Muslims changed the notion of "welcoming" from a voluntary ideal, by which a religion's availability would be made known and those who voluntarily chose to join would be welcomed, into a religious requirement for salvation. Coercion, violence, and bribery became matters of policy, not aberrations. The mission to force conversion, often practiced brutally against the Jews, made the very act of conversion seem unpleasant at best and deadly at worst. The Jewish and Gentile communities became more and more antagonistic, until Jews didn't see Gentiles as potential converts and Gentiles didn't see Judaism as a religion worthy of being embraced.

3. The fate of conversion in *halachah* followed its fate in communal perception, social ideology, and history. The commentators who taught halachah in France and Germany in the second half of the thirteenth century (exemplified by Rashi and the Tosafists) favored welcoming converts. Indeed, the Tosafists understood such welcoming as basic to Judaism. The halachic decision-makers centered in North Africa and Spain (exemplified by such scholars as Simeon Kayyara, Isaac Alfasi, and Maimonides) were more restrictive in their view of actively welcoming, although not hostile toward, righteous converts. There were various attempts to balance those two approaches, concluding in the authoritative code by

Joseph Caro, the *Shulchan Arukh* (1564–65), which has a mixed attitude toward conversion. Caro presented the laws of conversion more favorably than did the decision-makers but evidently did not see welcoming converts as a commandment, as did the commentators. The understanding of a conversionary obligation in Jewish law slowly withered.

It is now time to reclaim the original Jewish obligation to welcome converts. Such efforts do not endanger Jewish lives anymore. The competitors against Judaism in the modern world have failed; there is a spiritual hunger, and many people currently unattached to a religion would find Judaism congenial. A creative but traditional reading of halachah allows for the resumption of such an obligation. Finally, after the creation of the nation of Israel, there is a center from which the light unto the nations can emanate.

Indeed, if the Jewish people's heroic efforts can recreate a holy nation after almost 2,000 years of exile, that great people can resume its divine obligation to offer the message of Judaism and welcome those who choose to join the Jewish people on their historic spiritual journey.

Let me now consider how welcoming converts helps respond to the contemporary problem of Jewish continuity.

Welcoming converts to Judaism is frequently seen as making the best of a bad social trend. At the time of this writing, the large number of intermarriages between Jews and Gentiles are marginally diminished by the 5 percent of Gentile spouses who convert to Judaism. Meanwhile, the ongoing debate remains focused on how best to encourage Jewish continuity and whether or not to target some communal funds toward the intermarried or those already attached to Jewish life.

Lost in such a debate is not only how encouraging conversion can turn intermarried families into Jewish families but also how such encouragement can contribute to Jewish continuity. Beyond the current relatively modest demographic contribution (which, of course, includes increased political power and philanthropic giving for the Jewish community), welcoming converts helps Jewish continuity in four crucial ways: It (1) provides a way to reach the Jewish romantic partner of many converts; (2) increases the worth of Judaism in the eyes of born Jews; (3) brings into the community people who value religion as the core of Jewish experience and who, therefore, can complement American Jews who see ethnicity, culture, or nationality as the core of Jewish life; and (4) identifies a specific Jewish mission to provide a post-Zionist purpose to American Jewish life.

An effort to encourage conversions among the intermarried will identify not only interested Gentiles who wish to embrace Judaism, but also interested Jews who are currently intermarried. That is so because some Jews who are intermarried retain a strong Jewish identity; they simply fell in love with someone who was not born Jewish. Indeed, their potent Jewish identity is one reason why their spouses may have considered conversion in the first place. Because converts often have Jewish partners who maintain a continuing or rediscovered interest in intensifying their Jewish lives, these born Jews constitute a significant group for the Jewish community to reach. This can be done through such efforts as offering adult education courses and encouraging the born Jews to increase Jewish religious practices and to enhance their connections to the Jewish community. What is crucial to note is that it is the born-Gentile spouses who convert to Judaism who form the link between their born-Jewish spouses and the Jewish community. The convert serves as a marker, a way of identifying which intermarried born Jews remain interested in maintaining ties to the Jewish community. Similarly, programs aimed at conversion candidates or new converts along with their partners will be the programs most likely to attract born Jewish spouses.

Of course, not all Jewish spouses of converts fit this model. Some remain indifferent or even hostile to Judaism. Yet, because many conversion classes require Jewish partners to attend those classes, some of these Jews discover that their perception of Judaism had been formed and frozen through adolescent eyes and that seeing Judaism as an adult can and often does bring a more mature appreciation of a Jewish heritage.

One goal of continuity is to make Judaism itself more attractive to those now a part of the Jewish community. The principal method for accomplishing this goal is to structure institutional Jewish life in such a way as to make it exciting for those who already are a part of that life. However, it is also important that committed Jews receive messages that their free choice to remain as Jews in a society that allows and even encourages changing identities, including a religious identity, is a valid and worthwhile choice. One way that Jews can receive such a message is to see those not born Jewish want to become Jewish.

Advertisers understand this concept perfectly. When advertisers try to sell a product, their advertisements have two purposes: to lure new customers to purchase and use the product, but also to target current consumers of the product. The message to those current consumers is that the product they use is attractive, in fact so attractive that other people want it. Similarly, efforts to attract newcomers to Judaism simultaneously send a message to practicing Jews that Judaism is a desirable religious identity. When people do embrace Judaism, their joining the Jewish people validates for born Jews the worth of Judaism and contributes to the value of the identity they have chosen to retain.

People who convert to Judaism most frequently cite Judaism's sensible religious beliefs and attractive practices as the reason for their conversion. The ethnic, cultural, or national identities that are at the heart of the identities of most born Jews in the United States are sometimes perplexing both for converts and the Jewish communities they join. Converts see Judaism's crucial attraction as religious and must struggle to understand Judaism's ethnic dimensions.

Some born Jews cling to the misguided notion that converts can never be truly Jewish because Jewishness is a biological or cultural status. Indeed, some who oppose spending time and funds to welcome converts cite the legitimate danger that because converts see Judaism as primarily religious they are unable to assimilate fully into the Jewish people and thus can't truly transmit their Judaism to their children, making them one-generation converts. Similarly, opponents who see Judaism as primarily cultural or national see those who view Judaism as solely religious as transforming Judaism into a more Protestant-style religion with people divided into belief groups.

Clearly, converts do need help in absorbing an ethnic identity, which involves learning Jewish culture, developing a Jewish consciousness so as to see and feel as a Jew, and structuring a connection to Israel. Yet converts themselves want such help.

Part of the problem is the complexity of defining a Jewish identity. That identity contains separate elements, but simultaneously these elements are part of a single, united entity. In that sense, Judaism is like a tapestry with many individual threads. Some people see a prominent thread they find attractive and define Judaism as exclusively that thread. They are not incorrect in seeing the thread as genuinely Jewish, but are incorrect in identifying the thread as identical to all of Judaism. Seeing Judaism as a religion is, of course, totally correct but also incomplete. Judaism's tapestry essentially forms a religious design, and religion is the major thread. However, there are other significant threads, and a full conception of Judaism has to include such threads as ethnicity, culture, and nation. In this sense, converts need to learn more about Judaism than its religious beliefs and practices.

But if converts have in part failed to establish ethnic, cultural, or national connections, too often the Jewish community has not established the structures to help complete the conversion from simply the religious to include the many threads of a Jewish identity. That is, the Jewish community needs to develop institutional ways to add ethnicity, culture, and nationality to a convert's Jewish identity.

Too often overlooked, however, is that the problem of converts absorbing an ethnic, cultural, and national identity can be turned around. If converts come to Judaism too often focused exclusively on a religious identity, their incomplete notion of Judaism is mirrored by a similarly incomplete notion by many born Jews who see Judaism as only an ethnicity or a culture or a nation and do not adequately focus on religion as the center of Jewish identity.

Indeed, it could be argued that it was the very absence of a religious identity in many born Jews, a religious identity that carries with it a sense of divine obligation, that made ethnically conscious American Jewry susceptible to the lures of America and Gentile romantic partners.

That is, as converts absorb an ethnic identity they can contribute to Jewish continuity by passing on their religious fervor to their ethnic, cultural, and nationalist born-Jewish teachers. Both groups will find their Jewishness deepened by the encounter and both groups will be more likely to have children who will continue as Jews.

Continuity also requires purpose. For Jews to continue as Jews across the generations they must have a transcendent reason for doing so. Jewish history has frequently supplied American Jews with secular goals; reducing anti-Semitism, freeing Soviet Jews, and aiding Israel have been the most prominent. These three goals have substantially been met. American Jewry finds itself without a clear goal and in need of one.

Such a goal needs to be grounded in Jewish thought and history, solve a principal social problem facing Jews, and connect the two, so that direct action to solve the problem carries with it a transcendent purpose. Encouraging conversion to Judaism and welcoming those who do join the Jewish people provides such a purpose.

Such a purpose is grounded in Jewish sacred literature. For example, in the Talmud Rabbis Johanan and Elezar ben Pedat (B.T. Pesachim 87b) assert that God exiled the Jews from their sacred homeland and set them in the diaspora for only one purpose: to increase the number of converts. As previously noted, it is a striking notion that so horrible an event as exile should be seen to have a divine use. The use (seeking converts) had to have been considered so valuable that it justified exile from the land promised by God. At various crucial times in Jewish history, from Abraham and Sarah "gathering souls" to the absorption of many converts especially during the Second Temple Period, pre-medieval Jewish history is punctuated with Jewish communities welcoming converts. The nature and extent of their missionary efforts and successes is a matter of intense scholarly dispute, but Jews did welcome converts to their midst during the formative years of Judaism's development.

Encouraging conversion and welcoming converts helps confront the social problem of intermarriage in that it radically transforms an intermarried family into a Jewish family. With sufficient numbers, that is, conversion can reduce the intensity of the effects of intermarriage upon American Jews. The extent to which conversion to Judaism can affect overall Jewish life remains uncertain until serious efforts are made by the Jewish community to attract converts.

Welcoming converts is not always seen as beneficial to the reduction of intermarriage. Some observers believe that as the Jewish community sends a message of welcome to potential converts, it also sends another message, a wrong message, to the born-Jewish young: interdating and intermarriage are all right because the born-Gentile spouse can always convert to Judaism. It is important not to send such a message, in large part because it is false. Clearly, currently only a small percentage of born-Gentiles romantically involved with a Jewish partner convert to Judaism. Therefore, it is not statistically likely that a Gentile partner will convert. Even with a conversion, of course, Jewish children will still encounter close family members (e.g., grandparents, aunts, uncles, cousins) who are Gentile, and those family members, unintentionally or not, can provide an alternative to a fully Jewish identity. Therefore, it is important for Jews not to argue that interdating is all right because the Gentile can convert.

Such a clear message, however, should not preclude an overall nuanced message. There also needs to be a message to the currently romantically involved. There are now about one million born Jews married to unconverted Gentile spouses. These families need to receive a clear message from the Jewish community that they are welcome in Jewish life. Clearly, the Jewish community has an interest in encouraging those families to raise their children as Jews and, when appropriate, to welcome those Gentile spouses interested in conversion to Judaism. This balanced message is not always easy, but to leave either part out is to present an incomplete response to intermarriage.

Another social problem Jews face is the general problem of diminishing numbers, a problem profoundly negatively affected by intermarriage. One way in which numbers can be partially replenished is through welcoming converts to Judaism who are not romantically involved with a Jewish partner. Many people are on a spiritual search and, for them, Judaism provides a comfortable spiritual path. It is common but misleading to think of these people as Christian. In fact, the overwhelming number of them have already had highly developed doubts about their birth religion and deliberately have embarked on a religious search. Judaism is only one of a variety of alternatives they typically explore. That is, when encouraging such seekers, Judaism is not competing with Christianity but with alternative spiritual paths or secularism.

Judaism does not claim that its followers have an exclusive ticket into heaven. This theological tolerance puts a brake on proselytism because righteous followers of other religions, such as Christianity, are not seen as in need of being saved. Therefore, Judaism does not seek to convert Christians (or followers of other religions) into Jews. Judaism does remain hospitable to those who, of their own accord and without a current religion, are searching for a religious way of life. These seekers provide valuable contributions to the Jewish people and will help in continuing the Jewish way of life.

Welcoming converts is grounded in Jewish thought and history. It does contribute to solving social problems such as intermarriage and demographic losses. Welcoming converts connects the Jewish heritage to solving current problems. For all these reasons, welcoming converts can function as the transcendent purpose needed in American Jewish life.

Sincere converts make enormous contributions to Jewish continuity. The Jewish community, not always recognizing these contributions, needs to re-calibrate its continuity strategy to include more efforts to welcome converts to Judaism.

American Jews are facing a crisis of purpose. They are unsure about the appropriate mission for their communal life. That purpose should be to welcome converts to Judaism.

The current crisis has come as a surprise. American Jews have, for almost half a century, been able and satisfied to define their purpose as solving the most serious Jewish problems. This purpose has provided both a useful and an interesting identity, and it proved important for Jewish survival and for the continuity of an American Jewish communal self.

Those Jewish problems that have been faced, and to a large extent actually solved, include aiding in Israel's birth and security and combatting anti-Semitism domestically and around the world. In addition, Jews have tried to ameliorate American societal ills by supporting various social causes.

Of course, many religious Jews already have a specifically Jewish purpose: fulfilling God's commandments. However, the vast majority of American Jews, bereft of this traditional understanding of Jewish purpose, have looked elsewhere. Some have found such a purpose outside Jewish life completely and have attached their conscience and drive to a general social or political cause.

Most American Jews, however far they have traveled from the orthodoxy of their grandparents, have retained some sense of religious allegiance and an even greater sense of pride. They were not prepared to jettison a Jewish identity for a nondescript political one. Neither, however, were they prepared to ground their Jewish identity in daily religious ritual. Instead, they have focused on social and political problems that Jews have faced. The Biblical commandments were transmuted into "commandments" to lobby the White House and Congress on behalf of Israel, to remember the Holocaust, to give to their local Federations, to educate against hate and for tolerance, and to support public and private efforts in a good-hearted attempt to eradicate poverty and disease.

This identity as solver of these problems, so useful to American Jewish self-definition, so valuable for so long in the quest for purpose, is no longer satisfying. One by one, all of the problems that have required American Jewish attention have ceased to be functional in providing a sense of purpose to American Jewish life because, like Israel, the problems have been essentially solved, or because, like anti-Semitism, the problems have been rendered far less dangerous, or because, as in the case of social activism, the traditional solutions are unpopular in the wider society, in large part because the problems have been much more widely perceived as not being susceptible to political solution.

Israel's very strength, its increasing trade, its ability to deal directly with American leaders, its lure for potential investors, its emerging sense of not wanting to be seen as a beggar, its resentment of American Jewish money and power, all have combined to reduce dramatically the effect American Jews have on Israeli life. The close ties between Israeli and diaspora Jews continue, of course, but those ties are undergoing a role reversal. Israel is seen as supporting and helping American Jewry in preserving a Jewish identity. The Zionist identity for American Jews is being replaced by an identity as frequent visitor, as student and traveler. This subtle change alters the locus of control in the relationship. It makes American Jews reliant on Israel, rather than on their own actions for Israel, as a source of identity.

Such a solution is unsatisfying; solely relying on Israel does not provide a purpose for American Jewish life unless such a reliance evolves into a drive for the mass migration of American Jews to Israel. It is unsatisfying because a trip, even an extended one, is by definition of limited duration. While it does nurture memory or even encourages transformation, it does not define daily activity, and activity, not memory or even metamorphosis, is what will form the identity of and provide the purpose for the pragmatic majority of American Jews.

Jews also have fought anti-Semitism and have successfully kept the memory of the Holocaust alive. However, remembering and honoring the dead and the survivors form a moral obligation, not an identity. These memories, sites, prayers, and recollections bring Jews together, unite them as a group, and provide emotional energy for continuing Jewish struggles. However, other than combatting contemporary anti-Semitism and other forms of hatred and continuing to remember, none of these provides a program of action. This lack of program is particularly crucial because of the nature of contemporary anti-Semitism.

Many American Jews still, to a surprising extent considering reality, consider themselves under siege from anti-Semites. Groups that combat anti-Semitism will remain strong for some time. But as the reality of the security of American Jewish life is matched by an accurate perception of that reality, an event that will most importantly take place with the passing of the oldest generation of American Jews and the emergence of the succeeding generation, contemporary anti-Semitism will be seen for what it is: an intermittent source of intense grief or irritation that must be fought and eliminated but not a threat and not frequent or profound enough to endanger the corporate existence of American Jewry. As these perceptions change, the sense of lachrymose endangerment will diminish and with it the utility of fighting anti-Semitism as a principal source of Jewish identity.

Similarly, international anti-Semitism seems, at least currently, to be waning. The major battles to allow the free emigration of Jews from the former Soviet Union and from Syria have been won. The problems that remain include terrorism in Israel and elsewhere, as exemplified by the recent horrific bombing in Argentina, as well as isolated acts of anti-Semitism, the potential resurgence of anti-Semitic regimes, and so on, but for the moment no large Jewish population's existence is communally endangered.

Finally, the recent large government programs aimed at social betterment have been unsuccessful, and at any rate they have no direct Jewish content. The widespread contempt for these programs and the concomitant efforts to dismantle or dramatically alter them continue to reduce or eliminate such efforts as providing a useful source for an American Jewish identity. While some, or even many, Jews continue to adhere to their basic desire to be active in social causes, the lack of opportunity to do so because of what is likely to be a defunding or radical alteration of the programs, the ineffectuality of those efforts, and a failure to separate these liberal efforts from specifically Jewish efforts make social activism decreasingly useful in providing the basis for a Jewish purpose.

The removal of pro-Israel activities, combatting anti-Semitism, and social activism as providing a Jewish purpose to life is creating a crisis in purpose for American Jews, a crisis that will deepen over the next few years as Israeli Jews separate more from American Jews, as anti-Semitism is seen as less of a threat, and as social programs decline in number.

This crisis has provoked the beginnings of reflection by American Jews on the meaning of their lives. Such a reflection allows for the posing of a meta-teleological question: What is the purpose of having a Jewish purpose to American Jewish life?

First of all, a purpose has to retain a part of the current definition by being a response to a perceived problem with a definite solution to that problem provided. Of course, a Jewish purpose must also be coherent with basic Jewish beliefs, history, tradition, and values.

A purpose comes from having a sense of mission. Most American Jews, for better or worse, are not in search of some transcendent mission, one coming from a divine command. Rather than a transcendent purpose, most American Jews seek what might be called a purpose based on meaning, a goal that infuses Jewish meaning into their lives. That meaning is most infused for them when they help endangered Jews. Their religious mission, their purpose, must involve acting in the social and political world to help Jews in trouble.

The search for such a purpose might usefully begin then with a survey of the major problems that endanger Jewish life and remain unsolved. It is these unsolved dangerous problems that can provide the basis for an American Jewish purpose.

While many problems can be considered, the major ones fall into two broad categories: problems of maintaining an adequate Jewish population and problems of retaining a Jewish identity in the United States.

For examples of the first group, consider two widely noted problems: intermarriage and assimilation. The concern among American Jews about intermarriage is a problem precisely because the core Jewish density is so low that when intermarriage reaches a high proportion (currently about 52 percent) there is a danger to the survival of the people. Intermarriage is a crucial way in which, over one or several generations, Jews leave Judaism. The dislike of intermarriage is not a case of hating Gentiles; it is a visceral fear that the Jewish population is diminishing to such an extent as to endanger communal survival. When the intermarriage rate was low, communal concern was low. There were concerns for the individual fates of the intermarrying Jews and their progeny, but not a concern for the community's continuity.

Assimilation is another problem faced by American Jews. Sometimes assimilation overlaps intermarriage, in that those Jews seeking to blend in with the culture do so more easily when they marry someone outside the Jewish faith. However, assimilation also has other meanings. It can mean, for example, the literal abandonment of Judaism for another religious faith or, much more commonly, no religious faith at all. It can mean a lack of Jewish observance, not affiliating with a Jewish congregation, not providing a Jewish education for one's children, not identifying one's self with the fate of the Jewish people. Over time assimilation leads to intermarriage, or abandonment or such total indifference to Judaism so as not to be Jewish in any way except by a formal definition. Assimilation, like intermarriage, is harmful not because particular individuals make particular life choices that the Jewish community finds disloyal but because, with enough assimilation, the Jewish community's overall numbers decrease.

It should be added that the backdrop of these concerns is a demographic shrinking of those American Jews who do not intermarry or assimilate. They do, however, marry late and have fewer children than their grandparents or their Gentile peers, they are older on the average than gentile Americans, and they are more geographically dispersed than at any time in this century.

In 1937, Jews constituted 3.7 percent of the U.S. population. By 1977, that had dropped to 2.7 percent. By 1992, the estimated 5,828,000 American Jews constituted 2.3 percent of the U.S. population. For professional pessimists, the Council of Jewish Federations' 1990 National Jewish Population Survey estimated that there were only about 4.3 million religious Jews, making up 1.9 percent of the U.S. population.

There is controversy about the birth rate. While everyone agrees that 2.1 children per Jewish family are needed to replace the population, there is disagreement about how many children contemporary Jewish families will ultimately have because those births occur late. Pessimists claim a birth rate of 1.5 children per American Jewish family, citing a variety of demographic studies done in the 1960s and 1970s, especially the National Jewish Population Study of 1970–71. Optimists cite what seems to be a recent increase in Jewish births and claim intermarriage rates are lower and less endangering than believed by the general Jewish community. However, even if the optimists are right about a relatively stable Jewish population, a dubious assumption, because of an increasing Gentile population Jews will still be an ever-decreasing proportion of the American population.

Demographic growth, or at least stability, is vital for American Jews. Diminishing numbers imperil the communal infrastructure. Fewer Jews means it will be more difficult, for instance, to continue the established Jewish purposes of helping Israel and fighting anti-Semitism: raise funds for needy institutions and individuals; find volunteers for worthwhile activities; maintain political influence; decrease the surviving Jews' sense of alienation, marginality, confused self-image, and self-hatred; provide a market for Jewish literature, art, and music; and provide for all the other elements that make for a thriving and surviving community.

It is not the case, of course, that American Jewry is literally committing slow demographic suicide. There are strong countertrends to the declining numbers: high Orthodox birth rates, bulging day schools and Jewish camps, revived interest in travel to Israel, and interest in adult education. In addition, there are significant questions to which we simply do not know the answers. How many Jews will never marry? What will the birth and intermarriage rates be in ten years? How much Jewish immigration will there be to the United States? There will, to be sure, always be an American Jewry.

The quality of Jewish life, however, depends ineluctably on the quantity of Jewish life. The question is not whether the Jewish community will exist but whether its existence will matter. Will American Jews be the Amish of the twenty-first century, a quaint group of people with peculiar customs who are visited as though they were a walking, talking museum? Or, rather, will Jews maintain a place in the American mind as specifically Jewish contributors to the national political debate and to the general culture?

It is necessary to have a sufficient Jewish population in order that American Jewish existence matters, to maintain that place within the American mind. Right now, the threat to that population base is the greatest threat facing American Jews as a corporate body.

There are a variety of ways to increase the Jewish population. The most obvious way, of course, is to argue for an increase in Jewish births. Pronatalist efforts in the Jewish community have been by-and-large educational, such as by articles or sermons, rather than economic, such as by increased day care or alterations in dues structures and fees in some Jewish communal institutions for large Jewish families. Such efforts have not succeeded, again for obvious reasons: urbanization, education (the more education in a family, the lower the birth rate), wealth (as a family's income rises, fertility declines), women working outside the home, delayed marriage, delayed first child, divorce, and so on. The failures of pronatalist efforts exist precisely because even the staunchest advocates of increasing birthrates are reluctant to suggest deliberately decreasing education or income, or to suggest that all Jewish women revert to a home and family pattern that existed several decades ago. It is, then, extremely difficult to develop a successful pronatalist policy.

There have been many efforts worldwide by numerous countries to increase their populations. After World War I, France, Italy, and Germany provided financial incentives and nationalistic enthusiasm for a fertility increase that, it turned out, they could not effect. Many East European nations such as Hungary, Czechoslovakia, and Rumania developed pronatalist policies in the 1960s that included paid maternity leaves, cash bonuses for births, taxes on childless couples, and so on, but there is no proof that such efforts led to a long-term increase.

In Israel, there is the famous case of David Ben-Gurion proposing that the Israeli government pay a cash bonus to every Israeli woman who gave birth to a tenth child. Since too many of those who collected were Arab—the government being required to give equal treatment—the plan was discontinued.

In summary, there is no evidence that a concerted private pronatalist effort to increase Jewish births will have any dramatic effect. While some demographers argue that very large economic incentives will work, the American Jewish community has, for now and the foreseeable future, neither the resources nor the inclination to test that theory.

There have also been other attempts to increase Jewish numbers in the United States. One of these efforts, far more successful than pronatalism, has been to welcome Jewish immigrants from abroad, especially from Israel and from nations where Jews have suffered persecution. The problem with relying on immigration is that an increase in immigration is not consonant with the views of most Americans. If anything, there is strong and growing political pressure to remove illegal immigrants and restrain immigration. In addition, any future Jewish immigrants have to compete against other immigrants. Finally, many American Zionists and Israeli officials believe that Jewish immigrants ought to be heading for Israel, not the United States. Therefore, while immigration has worked in the past as a way to increase or stabilize the Jewish population, its future potential is very much more limited.

Another effort to increase the Jewish population has been to redefine who is a Jew. By long-standing tradition, a Jew has been defined as someone born to a Jewish mother or who has legally converted to Judaism. In 1983, the Central Conference of American Rabbis, a Reform group, declared that children would be considered Jewish if either parent, mother or father, were Jewish and if the child publicly and formally identifies with the Jewish faith and people. Such a definition would increase the Jewish population by expanding inclusion to those not currently counted. However, currently Orthodox and Conservative Jews do not accept such patrilineal Jews as fully Jewish. Without such recognition, it remains unclear whether and if so how these people are to be counted as part of the Jewish community.

Another way to increase the Jewish communal population is for Jews to accept unconverted Gentiles into the Jewish community as full participants, for example, in familial, congregational, and organizational Jewish life. This counting in of Gentiles as part of Jewish life, of course, neatly eliminates the problem of intermarriage and potential population decline. The danger to such a solution is syncretism; the boundaries between Jew and Gentile are virtually erased by such a solution. Over time, this, too, will lead to an absorption of Judaism by the wider Christian culture.

One way to "increase" the population is to prevent a decrease through assimilation. Those who advocate this approach focus principally on education, Jewish experiences such as camps and trips to Israel, and encouraging a more family centered Jewish life. These preventative methods may indeed work. However, even if they are 100 percent effective (a claim no one is yet prepared to make), they will simply have eliminated the number of intermarriages and kept the Jewish community stable. There will be no real increase in population, only a reduction of the decrease. While this is certainly a worthy and valuable goal, and obviously should be vigorously pursued, it does not get to the problem of increasing Jewish numbers, especially because the aging Jewish population and the low fertility rates will decrease the numbers considerably, independent of assimilation and intermarriage.

Another way that Jews have increased their population is by adopting children who are not Jewish and raising them as Jews. Of course, population increase is rarely, if ever, the reason for adoption. Still, whatever the motive, adopting Gentile infants and children and raising them as Jews does increase the Jewish population. Adoption, however, is a limited option as a means to increase the Jewish population. There are many more people who wish to adopt children than there are babies to adopt. Additionally, the same economic and social reasons why relatively few children are adopted influence the fact that relatively few Jewish children are being born. Finally, because the idea of increasing the number of Jews by adoption presumes the adopted Gentile infant will be converted to Judaism, adoption is really one variant of another option for increasing the number of Jews: increasing the number of conversions to Judaism.

Welcoming converts to Judaism is the surest way to increase the Jewish population. Obviously, every new convert by definition increases the Jewish population.

Put simply in crude economic terms, terms which obviously do not express the central spiritual and social values of a convert, it would have been extremely expensive to raise 200,000 Jews in America. Converts save the Jewish community an enormous amount of money. In addition, the 200,000 converts become potentially active in the Jewish community as congregational members, donors to Jewish charities, volunteers, or in other ways. For instance, conversionary families, in a wide variety of studies, have been shown to be much more likely to donate to Jewish charities than have intermarried families. If conversionary families have more than 2.1 children, they increase the number of Jews in the world; in such a way one convert can contribute many more than one new Jew to the world, especially if the effect is seen after many generations.

However, the increase of Jews by conversion is also subtle. When the convert is romantically involved with a Jewish partner, the Jewish partner often does not become assimilated. Additionally, when that romantic relationship is in what would have been an intermarriage, the conversion makes it three times more likely that the children of the union will be raised as Jews. Again, every conversion not only adds one new Jew to the population, but it can add many others as well.

Conversion is important as a way to increase the Jewish population because of its vast potential. Are there large numbers of people who will convert to Judaism? The honest answer is that we just don't know. According to the CJF 1990 National Jewish Population Survey, there were 739,000 Jews who are currently married to unconverted Gentile spouses. There were 664,000 children in these mixed households, with only 25 percent of those children being raised as Jews. The 739,000 Gentile spouses, added to the 498,000 children in these mixed marriages not raised as Jews but having a Jewish parent, total almost one-and-a-quarter million people who are potential converts. (This number is not precisely accurate because some of the children in mixed marriages not being raised as Jews are legally Jewish because they have a Jewish mother. In their case, the aim is not religious conversion but a symbolic conversion to be raised and educated as Jews. Still, the number who could formally be converted is extraordinarily high.) Of course, since the 1990 study, the raw number of intermarriages has increased as has the number of children in those marriages.

Potential converts are not limited to the spouses or children of an intermarriage. At least 10 percent of those who convert to Judaism do so with no romantic attachment to a Jewish partner, but rather because of, for example, finding Judaism spiritually satisfying. These spiritual seekers had to find Judaism on their own, with no encouragement at all from a Jewish romantic partner or the Jewish community. It is unknown how many people currently unattached to a religion but actively searching for a satisfactory one, would be interested in Judaism if they knew that Judaism did welcome converts.

Several factors will determine whether Jews successfully get a large number of converts and increase the Jewish population. The various movements within Judaism will have to develop their institutional policies concerning actively seeking and welcoming converts and integrating them into the community. The movements will have to translate these policies into institutional structures. The policies and structures will have to be made widely known to the American Jewish and Gentile population. In part, the policy to increase conversions will affect the policy toward reaching out to the intermarried; seeking converts will have to be an explicit goal of such outreach.

The decline of the American Jewish population is not the only important problem facing American Jews. Other problems of the Jewish community center on how Jews can retain a Jewish identity in American society. These problems reflect the difficulty of balancing a Jewish and an American identity. American Jews face multiple dangers here, among which are: (1) an evaporation of Jewish identity by seeing Jews as "white" in a society defined by race; (2) an identity that must be freely chosen rather than communally enforced (there is no excommunication of errant Jews in America); and (3) the general psychological and social problems inherent in minority-group membership, such as a hypersensitivity to differences, accepting negative group stereotypes, and a feeling of marginality or even self-hatred. This last point underscores the fact that to some extent identity problems are also tied to demography because so many identity problems emerge from Jewish minority status. Additionally, if American Jews wanted to keep a separate identity, their rates of intermarriage and assimilation would decrease.

Finding a purpose is important for Jews in dealing with identity problems. Insofar as Jews have a purpose, the inherent tension between the Jewish and American parts of their identity will be more stable; the overwhelming intrusion of American life will not destroy a Jewish identity as long as a clear Jewish purpose is present and is powerful enough to resist the intrusion. The loss of purpose exacerbates the already existing problem of the maintenance of a separate Jewish identity.

Clearly, there are many traditional ways of maintaining that separate identity. Jewish education, especially day school education, is one. Joining and participating in Jewish congregations and performing more Jewish practices, especially in the home, is another. Providing Jews, young and old alike, with rich Jewish experiences in such places as in camps or on trips to Israel and other Jewish sites is a third way.

The problem with these traditional ways is that American Jews have known about them all along. Too many American Jews have rejected these traditional ways of keeping a separate Jewish identity, ignoring them and substituting other activities. With those activities disappearing and with the growing challenges for American Jews of intermarriage, assimilation, and maintaining a separate identity, many American Jewish leaders believe and hope that the traditional routes will become much more attractive to those American Jews, that the rejected options will, perhaps in desperation, be embraced.

They may be. If they were, American Jewry will radically enhance its chances for continuity and growth. Therefore, these traditional methods need to be supported financially and morally by the wider Jewish community.

The problem is, what if American Jews, now bereft of purposes to maintain a separate Jewish identity, don't turn back to these traditional ways, don't see them as providing a purpose for their lives? Is there also another supplemental purpose that can be added as a safeguard?

If seeking and welcoming converts is the best way to solve the demographic problem, can such an effort also provide the needed purpose for American Jews to retain their separateness in America?

In answering this question, it is useful to isolate what is attractive about supporting Israel and social causes and fighting anti-Semitism. While there may be various factors, one obvious factor is that in the case of Israel and anti-Semitism, there was a clear, easily defined, external threat to the physical survival of Jews. If, as has been suggested, problems clustered around demographic survival are the major threat to Jewish survival, and seeking converts is the best response to that threat, then seeking converts can clearly provide the needed purpose.

This must, however, be an ambivalent assertion because intermarriage, assimilation, and identity concerns are not seen as an analogous major threat to Jewish survival by a wide enough number of American Jews (as opposed to wide numbers of American Jewish rabbis and communal leaders who definitely see these as a threat). The attack on Israel in 1967 or the struggle for freedom by Jews in the former Soviet Union were much more clearly seen as threats, in large part because there were both villains Jews could easily define and victims with whom Jews could easily identify. The struggle against demographic dangers is a struggle by-and-large against an abstract idea. The only possible "villains" in this struggle are those Gentiles who marry Jews, and virtually all of them are good people who have fallen in love, hardly appropriate candidates for demonization.

If we can't focus on "villains" in providing a human face to the demographic problem, we have to focus on the "victims"—those Jews who intermarry and assimilate, losing their Jewish identity. In seeing such Jews as victims, we need to compare the demographic losses from intermarriage, assimilation, and loss of identity to physical losses from anti-Semitism. Indeed, viewing such Jews as victims will make it easier to sympathize with them and not to see them as betrayers of Jewish tradition. The Jewish community will have to picture a photo of a large Jewish family with individuals, one by one, disappearing from the photo.

In dealing with such demographic losses by seeking converts, Jewish activity can be compared to social activism. Aiding in the demographic growth of Jews is a way for Jews to do something to improve the world. In addition, it is potentially effective social activism because demography is often susceptible to human decision, and intermarriage, assimilation, and identity problems are, to some considerable extent, a problem internal to the Jewish community and so not dependent on outside powers. The same photograph will have to be seen differently, with some of those who were lost staying while others who are gone being replaced with new people.

Besides solving the demographic problems caused by Jewish intermarriage and assimilation, and aiding in solving the identity problem, seeking converts has other virtues as well as its candidacy for an appropriate Jewish purpose. Seeking and welcoming converts is an activity, providing American Jews with specific actions to take in the wider society. It has a mechanism for evaluating its own success or failure by calculating how many people are converted and how many of those affiliate with a Jewish congregation or organization. It is coherent with Jewish values and traditions. It strengthens the identity of Jews by forcing them to learn enough about Judaism to offer it to others. It weakens the arguments of those who claim that Judaism is particularist or exclusionary. It brings into the Jewish community people from a religious background, making religion, as opposed to ethnicity, more prominent in Jewish life, a factor which can help reinvigorate American Jewish religious life.

This last point is important because it provides a bridge to the more traditional segments of American Jewry. Those traditional Jews, too, need to see a specifically religious purpose to welcoming converts beyond the prudential reasons for combatting intermarriage. Such a religious reason exists if seeking converts can be seen as it once was—a religious obligation central to the Jewish enterprise in history. Such an idea of religious mission, summed up, is that the entire Jewish people, divinely chosen, having freely accepted a covenant with God that included missionary obligations, has the spiritual vocation to bear witness to Judaism and to bring God's universal moral message to all humanity by offering their faith, and to welcome converts who accept the particularities of the moral message. Jews were very active proselytizers, especially during and immediately after the Second Temple Period. Over time, a tradition of discouraging converts slowly developed. The prudential reasons for such discouraging made sense at the time, because the Jewish community and the converts were severely punished by Roman, Christian, and Moslem authorities. The gap between Jew and Christian grew so wide that it became difficult to see a Christian as interested in converting. Jewish law naturally reflected such an atmosphere, and so, unsurprisingly, it eventually favored a very circumspect approach to welcoming or even accepting converts. It is this legacy of diaspora Jewish life that many traditional Jews have inherited. It is unclear whether such an inheritance can be overcome to claim the earlier inheritance of a positive attitude toward converts. The theological and historical roots are there for such an attempt.

It remains, then, a vital effort for American Jewish leaders to identify and define the major unsolved problems in Jewish life, to translate those problems into concrete terms that are easily grasped, to communicate those problems to the wider Jewish public, and, together, to identify the best ways for those problems to be solved. In addition to the traditional ways, the best way to provide a much-needed purpose in American Jewish life is for Jews to reclaim their ancient role as a light unto the nations.

In spite of all the positive aspects of welcoming converts, activities to promote such welcoming continue to be assailed. Let us consider some of the arguments used to say that Jews should not welcome converts. Anyone who has dealt with conversion for a long time has heard many dramatic stories. Often the stories are tremendously joyful. There are, in addition to such stories, many sad ones as well, of people who want to convert but who wish to continue praying to the Christian saints. One story I heard involves a rabbi counseling a woman considering conversion. He could tell that the woman had very mixed feelings, so he suggested they study some more but wait for the conversion. One day, by accident, he saw her coming out of a church. Stammering, she told him that she went there to pray. The conversion, of course, did not take place.

There are stories of emotionally overwhelmed parents who can't accept their child's becoming Jewish, or of Jewish parents who can't accept their child's marriage to anyone not born Jewish.

Here are two extended stories about such cases.

They were like any young couple in love. Sam and Cathy wanted to get married. It seemed so easy, so simple a matter of making their private love public, until they told their parents.

Sam's Jewish parents offered him $10,000 to forget Cathy. He refused to consider the possibility and, eventually, his parents decided they could accept Cathy if Sam agreed to spend two years in Israel studying with a rabbi. At first, Sam also refused this demand, but his parents persisted. "You are both young, and this will be a test of your love. If she waits for you and still wants to marry you, then you will have our blessing." Sam went to Cathy with the idea. They discussed it, and finally, reluctantly, they agreed.

Cathy's Protestant family wasn't happy either. Her father, a minister, joined the family in making threats. The possibility of Cathy's conversion to Judaism was raised, but it was made clear that such an option would not be accepted.

Both families met to discuss what they jointly called "the great problem." Cathy particularly noticed Sam's sister, "a sassy, spoiled little brat." No resolution emerged from the meeting, except that everyone thought the idea of Sam going to Israel was wonderful.

Cathy drove him to the airport on the day he was to leave. They embraced and swore eternal love. Sam sat on the plane and wrote Cathy a letter.

When he got to Israel, he continued to write every day. He never received a reply to those letters and so, desperate, Sam wrote to his family asking them to investigate. They agreed and wrote back saying Cathy was "out of town."

Unable to restrain himself after two months of hearing nothing, Sam returned to the United States to search for the woman he loved. He rushed to her house, only to be told by her parents that she was vacationing in Europe. They had told her such a trip would be helpful in getting her mind off her problem. They assured Sam that she would write him when she learned his address.

Sam left several of his letters for her. He journeyed back to Israel, awaiting word. It never came. Not a single letter from Cathy arrived.

Several months later, Sam got a letter from his parents. They told him very matter-of-factly that Cathy had married an old friend from school. Sam's mother suggested that Cathy was expecting a child.

Pained, uncertain about what to do, Sam finally flew back home again in search of Cathy. He went to see Cathy's parents. They told him to leave, but he refused to do so without learning where he could find Cathy. The parents called the police. Suddenly, Sam and Cathy's father began to fight. Thinking back, Sam reflects, "If the police had not arrived, I think I would have killed him with my bare hands. I was depressed, suicidal. Inside, I was like human driftwood."

Angry, unhappy, Sam did not know what to do except return to Israel. He found a cheap apartment in Jerusalem. The landlady, an older woman with three young sons, was a widow whose husband had been killed by Arabs eight years earlier.

Sam worked hard all day. At night he drank himself to sleep. One evening he returned home and found the landlady waiting in his bed. He resisted, but her campaign to seduce him continued.

She would introduce him as her "husband." When Sam's parents came to visit, she embraced them warmly. His parents liked the woman. Sam says of those days, "I was not living; I was existing."

He yearned each moment to know what had happened to Cathy.

He would have been shocked had he learned the truth.

Cathy had returned home from the airport after dropping Sam off for his trip. Her parents had "a great idea," they told her. Why not go to Europe to get her mind off her "love-struck heart." They promised to forward all of Sam's letters. Cathy loved museums and art, and so decided as long as she couldn't see Sam anyway, that the trip could be a way to pass the time.

Cathy went, and waited for the letters, which never came. Cathy wrote to her parents, but they told her that Sam had never bothered to write any letters. Cathy wouldn't believe it. She wrote to all her friends, but no one knew where Sam was.

Cathy returned home, and her parents told her the news. Sam had gotten married in Israel and would not be returning. Cathy went to see Sam's parents and sister. The parents confirmed the marriage and told Cathy how happy Sam was. They refused to give her his address because they did not think it was proper.

It took a year of searching for Cathy to discover Sam's address. She wrote a letter, but did not mail it. "I was hurt and bleeding on the inside. My dreams had been shattered. I no longer believed in love."

Cathy changed jobs, but that didn't help. Her parents tried to find someone for her to marry, but when she met those prospective love interests, she "made no effort to be nice or charming. In fact, I was rude and indifferent." However, Cathy's mother planned a marriage for her to the son of one of their friends. Cathy never told her poor future husband that she loved him.

Cathy did get married. She and her husband slept in separate beds on their honeymoon. On her wedding night, repulsed by her husband, Cathy vomited.

The marriage lasted for four months before it was annulled.

Again adrift, Cathy rented a store and began selling hobby books. The time passed.

Four years after she had kissed Sam good-bye at the airport, Cathy was working in her store when the phone rang. It was Sam's sister. Cathy was shocked to hear from her because the two had never gotten along.

The truth came pouring out. Sam was coming back to the United States. He had written more than fifty letters, but the parents of both couples had joined together to destroy or hide the letters. Sam had never really married. Instead, he had been told that Cathy was married with two children and had moved to California.

Cathy sat down and cried. "The tears would not stop," she recalls. Sam's sister said she would bring her brother directly from the airport to see Cathy. On the trip, she would tell Sam the truth.

Cathy closed the store, barricading herself inside. She paced back and forth for four hours.

Then the knock came. Sam had arrived. For an hour they did nothing but hold each other and embrace, each refusing to let go of the other. Later, they began to talk, crying together "out of hurt and happiness."

The two, so in love, had never been intimate. They drove to a hotel, where they again declared their love for each other.

In the morning Cathy awoke and quickly reached over to make sure Sam was still there. "The nightmare was over. The dream had begun," she says.

A mild breeze wafted through the open window, gently swaying the blue damask curtains.

Lying there in bed, Cathy decided that it was on that day that she would tell Sam the secret. Two weeks after he had left for Israel she had secretly begun her conversion to Judaism.

Devorah Wigoder was born with the name Jane McDwyer. Educated in a convent, sister of both a priest and a nun, Devorah faced a pained parent when she decided to convert.

It was long after her conversion. Devorah was living in Israel with her well-known husband, Geoffrey Wigoder. One day in 1956 she received a telegram from her brother, the priest. He told her that their mother was dying in a New York hospital. Her brother pleaded with Devorah not only to visit, but to re-convert to Catholicism. Such a move, her brother suggested, would ease their mother's deathbed pain. She wished to stay in Israel because of the difficult times there, but her husband urged her to visit her mother and told her the conversion issue was hers to decide.

She knew she was being asked to choose between her mother's dying feelings and the religion she cherished. She flew through the night, constantly praying for a way out of her dilemma. She arrived at the airport. Her brother was there, waiting to help her through a re-conversion ceremony. Instead, Devorah went directly to see her mother. She walked into the room, tiptoed to the bed. Her mother was sleeping as Devorah looked down at the kind face. Somehow her mother felt a presence and woke up.

"Jane! Jane! My child! Jane, what is this radiance that glows around you?"

"It is the Jewishness in me, Mother."

"If that is so, then God bless you, my saintly child!"

Devorah and her mother clung to each other and wept. Her mother died the next day and then Devorah began to write a book about her life, *Hope Is My House* (Englewood Cliffs, NJ: Prentice-Hall, 1966).

These dramatic stories swirl around the potential and actual convert, center on a spiritual search or an intermarriage, and put the focus on those born Gentile and their relationship to the Jewish community.

But arguments about conversion don't only take place in homes where there is a person considering becoming Jewish. Many born Jews have conflicting feelings about converts. In many ways, born Jews want to be welcoming, realizing at least in the abstract, that they should be.

However, many born Jews I have spoken with have, often reluctantly, voiced nagging doubts about welcoming converts. Sometimes these doubts center around serious issues, such as the disagreement about who is allowed to perform conversions, the appropriate procedures, the allowable motives for conversion, and so on. Another serious concern is that welcoming converts might imply an endorsement of a born Jew marrying someone not Jewish as long as a conversion occurs, which these critics believe reduces the Jewish objection to intermarriage. There are other serious concerns as well, such as that welcoming converts will increase anti-Semitism as discussed in a previous chapter; that money and time should be given to the education of born Jews, not to welcoming converts, or that such welcoming will lead to increased proselytizing by Christian groups.

Other doubts, however, are less substantive. Some born Jews doubt that a convert is really a Jew, or could ever be one. Some born Jews I have spoken with believe the Jews form a unique gene pool, and that somehow this alleged gene pool will be negatively altered by the addition of Gentiles.

Both sorts of doubts need to be openly discussed. No lingering doubts or fears about converts should remain unexpressed and undiscussed. The renewed Jewish act of welcoming converts is still so recent, so attached in the born-Jewish mind not to a covenantal obligation but to the troubling issue of intermarriage, that it would be absolutely amazing if those doubts did not exist.

Even well-meaning supporters of welcoming converts can admit to uncertainty. One rabbi, internationally famous and a passionate supporter of welcoming converts, once asked me if I had any converts in my family. I said I didn't, that my wife was born into a very devout Jewish home and my children were too young to marry, and that, so far as I knew, there were no converts among my wife's ancestors or mine (unless one goes back to Abraham). He said it was the same situation in his family, though some children were already married to born Jews. He then wondered aloud whether we would be so open and welcoming if we really had to be. We both agreed we hoped we would, and I think we both would be, but the observation is telling. It will take several generations of welcoming converts for all born Jews to see it as a natural part of Jewish life. Part of integrating such a view into the Jewish consciousness involves understanding welcoming as a divinely mandated activity, not just a pragmatic reaction to historical and social circumstance. Part involves educating born Jews. Finally, part involves really dealing with the emotional and intellectual conflicts about conversion.

It is, therefore, important to look at least at some of the major objections to welcoming converts.

Seeking Converts Causes Divisions among Jewish Denominations

As discussed in the chapter on intermarriage, it is clear that there is considerable truth to this objection. However, it is misleading to maintain that divisions between Orthodox and non-Orthodox movements in American Jewry would dissolve if no conversions at all took place. (Of course it should be understood that "Orthodox" here is used only to designate a position that is widely held among Orthodox movements and adherents. Not all Orthodox Jews subscribe to the positions ascribed to Orthodoxy here. A similar caveat must be entered in any discussion of "Conservative" and "Reform" Judaism as well.)

Ultimately, of course, from an Orthodox point of view, the modern rift in Judaism was caused when some Jewish religious rebels claimed that the *halachah* was no longer binding or that it was inherently evolutionary so that it could legitimately be changed, or that the written Torah was not given directly to Moses at Mount Sinai but composed by many figures over a long period of time, or that the oral Torah was not given at Sinai. From a non-Orthodox point of view, the rift was caused because Orthodoxy clung to a belief system and way of life that had been overtaken by modernity or because Orthodoxy misunderstood the fundamental adaptability of halachah. In doing so, this position concludes, and by claiming sole legitimacy, Orthodoxy found itself unable to adapt to the pluralism that characterizes contemporary Jewish life.

These fundamental differences over Judaism led to more and more problems, such as whether the rules of keeping kosher still applied, whether it was permitted to drive an automobile to services on Shabbat, what roles women have in religious life, and many others.

In this sense, conversions are not the cause of the dissension between Orthodox and non-Orthodox movements, but a sign of it.

However, in many ways, conversion is a more serious problem because those the Orthodox perceive as non-halachic converts are not considered to be Jewish at all, while non-observant born Jews are at least still considered Jewish. The Orthodox position is that such converts could not, under any circumstance short of another, halachic, conversion, be seen as legitimately Jewish and suitable, for instance, as marriage partners. Additional problems involving conversion include: (1) The Orthodox do not recognize the halachic authority of non-Orthodox rabbis to perform conversions. In general, the Orthodox recognize a conversion as legitimate when it occurs under the auspices of a *bet din*, a religious court, presided over by people who have a full knowledge of halachah and are fully observant. One general argument is that non-Orthodox rabbis either don't adhere to Jewish law, or do not accept that the written Torah and the oral Torah were given at Mount Sinai. (2) The Orthodox strictly adhere to a set of procedures that at least some Reform do not follow, such as a requirement for circumcision. (3) The Orthodox generally believe that only a strictly religious motive (independent, say, of a romantic attachment to a Jewish partner) is acceptable. There is considerable discussion among the Orthodox about such a position, and it is not universally held. (4) The Orthodox believe that a convert must accept and live by all 613 commandments. A conversion performed even by an Orthodox rabbi that does not meet these requirements is not deemed to be halachically valid.

As serious as are the differences between movements regarding conversion, conversion is not the sole serious problem. Consider, for example, the question of patrilineality, a principle accepted by the Reform and Reconstructionist movements. According to this principle, a child of a Jewish father and non-Jewish mother is considered Jewish if the child is raised as a Jew and makes public declarations of an intention to be Jewish. This, of course, runs counter to the traditional position, maintained by the Orthodox and Conservative movements, that only a child of a Jewish mother is automatically (that is, without a conversion) Jewish. Precisely the same problems of Jewish status that emerge in conversions also emerge in discussions of patrilineality. These problems also emerge in discussions of marriages that end with a civil divorce, but not a religious one, especially when the partners remarry and have children.

These, and other, issues remind us that the arguments about the Orthodox and non-Orthodox movements are grounded in fundamental philosophical differences, have played out for many generations across many issues, and include a variety of very serious problems, with conversion being only one among many.

This is not to say that the problem should be ignored. There are creative possibilities for solving conversionary issues within a halachic framework (such as joint religious courts, giving non-Orthodox children an Orthodox conversion at birth, or coming up with an agreement about appropriate procedures and requirements for conversion).

If seeking converts is seen as a divine obligation, these problems, difficult as they may be, should not be allowed to halt the continued search for converts. Additionally, the problems are internal to the Jewish community, not subject to outside force, and so require study and cooperation to solve.

Seeking Converts Makes Intermarriages Permissible

This objection requires some initial clarification. If we define an intermarriage as a marriage between someone who is Jewish and someone who is not, then when a conversion takes place prior to the marriage there is no intermarriage.

Sometimes sociologists, using a variety of terms, distinguish among intermarriage (marriage between two people of different religions), in-marriage (marriage between two people of the same religion), and mixed-marriage (marriage between two people who were born into two different religions). In this sense, even if a conversion occurs, a mixed-marriage, though not an intermarriage, takes place. It is, however, important to note that by Jewish law a conversion makes the convert fully and completely Jewish, so that the concept of mixed-marriage is a sociological, but not a religious, term.

Still, as Jews struggle to strengthen Jewish families and emphasize the importance of in-marriage, there is a sense that seeking converts makes it acceptable to date and agree to marry someone born Gentile so long as that person is willing to convert.

But welcoming converts is not a signal of acceptance to marry a born Gentile. If signals are sent by the community about the acceptability of marriage partners, those signals are sent far more strongly and much earlier than views about welcoming converts. If signals sent by parents, relatives, friends, teachers, rabbis, and congregants are abundantly clear that intermarriage is not acceptable, the message will be understood.

If conversion were tantamount to community acceptance of potential intermarriages, then many more conversions would be taking place. Accepting converts does not send a powerful signal to young Jews that intermarriage is acceptable.

There are many arguments that the Jewish community can use to foster Jews marrying someone born Jewish. These include: (1) potential problems can develop for the convert and the children (if the convert is female), had the conversion been performed by a non-Orthodox rabbi; (2) the extended family of the convert might have non-Jewish influences; and (3) a marriage's stability is usually enhanced when the couple share backgrounds, so that two born Jews usually have more in common than a born Jew and a born Gentile.

While in-marriage may be the ideal, in fact many born Jews fall in love and wish to marry people who are born Gentile. It is in such cases that the community must make a choice about whether accepting converts increases such relationships or simply increases the number of Jewish marriages.

Ultimately, people's motives for marrying are difficult if not impossible to fathom. Still, the acceptance of converts is, in fact, a correct signal; the normative Jewish view is that someone Jewish should marry someone else who is Jewish.

The Money and Efforts Used to Seek Converts Would Be More Useful If Spent on Keeping Born Jews Jewish

There is no inherent contradiction between trying to prevent born Jews from assimilating and seeking converts. Both efforts are vital; both are mandated by Judaism.

Indeed, it is the case that seeking converts will actually help in preventing assimilation. The reason for this is that people want what they see other people want.

This is most understandable using a commercial metaphor and comparing Judaism to a product. Obviously, this is unfair to Judaism, which is a serious religion, but the comparison is illuminating. An advertiser prepares messages about a product for two reasons. One reason is to attract new customers (comparable to converts). The other reason is to reassure current consumers of the product (born Jews) that the product they use is valuable. When people see ads for products they use, they receive reinforcement that their choice was correct.

It is also morally important to consider the alternative to seeking converts. Currently, for instance, there are more than 900,000 born Jews who are intermarried, that is, whose spouse and children have not converted. Focusing solely on preventing intermarriage effectively writes off these people, and all their future offspring, from the Jewish community. Such a stance is religiously and ethically untenable.

Finally, seeking converts does not have to drain resources from the Jewish community. Obviously, new converts bring in resources, such as money and volunteer time. Almost every rabbi I have spoken to about conversion has stories to tell about converts who are now Sisterhood presidents, or who are in other significant leadership positions in congregations and Jewish organizations. Additionally, seeking converts does not necessarily cost large amounts of money, which, in any case, might come from people interested in this cause but who do not give to other Jewish causes. Some no-cost or low-cost activities are discussed in the final section of this book.

Seeking Converts Will Encourage Christian Efforts to Convert Jews

Recently, a noted Jewish newspaper editor wrote to me saying that it was his understanding that there was an unwritten agreement with the national Christian religious organizations that if they do not actively enter into a conversion program for Jews, then the Jewish groups will not launch any public programs for converts. The implication of such an agreement, if it exists, is that, should Jews actively seek converts, in the ensuing competition for converts the vastly outspent and outnumbered Jewish community would inevitably lose.

I do not know if there if there is, in fact, such an agreement, but if there is, I wish someone would tell the many Christian groups that very actively seek specifically Jewish converts. That is, the competition is already taking place by some on one side, but not by anyone on the Jewish side. In addition to such active proselytizing, Jews, as a very small minority group in an overwhelmingly Christian nation, are subject to day-in and day-out assimilatory pressures. This is, perhaps, most evident at Christmas, with its endless supply of Christian-oriented television programs and public exhibitions and celebrations.

Any Jewish conversionary effort would therefore be simple self-defense against what is already occurring. Additionally, the methods favored by those in the Jewish community who wish to seek converts do not include going after Christians affiliated with their religion. Nor do they include intrusive efforts that interfere with the privacy or personal autonomy of other people. That is, even if more massive Jewish efforts were undertaken, they would not be the sorts of activities that might be thought of in the Christian mind as missionary, such as soliciting converts by going door-to-door or challenging the religious legitimacy of other religions or warning of dire consequences for the soul after death if no conversion takes place.

Finally, Reform Jewish efforts to win converts have been public knowledge for a decade and a half. Most Christians who have taken a stand on those efforts have, in fact, praised them. This is true in part because the activities are aimed at those without church affiliations, are unobtrusive, and are undertaken by a tiny group struggling for communal survival, and not by a group on the brink of converting millions of Christians.

For all these reasons, then, seeking converts would not lead to any additional proselytizing activities by American Christian organizations.

Converts Aren't Real Jews

Those who make this argument focus on the non-religious elements of Judaism as being unable to be absorbed by those not born Jewish. Theologically, all Jewish groups believe, in principle, that it is possible for someone born Gentile to convert to Judaism. Despite substantive differences among the different movements in Judaism, that is, there remains agreement on the theoretical possibility of conversion and its legitimacy, at least within the boundaries of each movement.

This argument, then, is really about Jewish culture. It is sometimes said that someone not born Jewish can't feel like a Jew, can't think like a Jew.

But no one at birth, born Jewish or not, knows what gefilte fish is, or has had the events of Jewish history seared into their consciousness, or can sprinkle some Yiddishisms into speech, or can pray. All culture is learned; emotional reactions are absorbed as well.

There is also the more unspoken assumption that perhaps Jews are smarter than others, that this intelligence provides a framework for analyzing the world. This presumed Jewish mind evidences itself in various sorts of intellectual achievement, whether in academia, business, entertainment, or elsewhere. In some respects this argument is part of the next one, that Jews have a special biological heritage that should not be tampered with. I will discuss such a view below.

Sometimes the belief that a convert can't really be a good Jew comes, ironically, from a species of Jewish self-hatred. Some people have such a low estimation of Judaism that they can't understand why people would want to become Jewish if they haven't had it thrust upon them at birth. For such people, Jews are trapped into their existence without a choice; being Jewish is seen as a condition of nature, not a voluntary spiritual choice. It is by now a cliche, however, that, at least in American Jewish life, all Jews are Jews by choice precisely because active assimilation through conversion to another religion or passive assimilation through indifference or intermarriage are free choices. Being Jewish is not a condition, but a choice. That choice is being made in two directions, by born Jews choosing to retain their Judaism and by converts choosing to become Jewish.

Jews Form a Unique Gene Pool

This view, that Jews form a biological group that is intelligent and accomplished and can only be harmed by the introduction of foreign elements, is, of course, obviously untrue. Any visitor to Israel, for instance, will see the very wide variety of people who are Jewish. The objector might then narrow the discussion to American (i.e., primarily Ashkenazic) Jewry. The unfortunate logic of such an argument is that Ashkenazic Jews should not only avoid converts as potential marriage partners but also non-Ashkenazic Jews, a position no Jew can take seriously.

Even if the biological argument is taken seriously, it can be argued that the introduction of new genes will contribute new and valuable strains to an already excellent gene pool. Anyone who has spoken to converts will attest to that possibility.

There is another variant to this argument. It is that the Bible refers to the "seed" of Abraham (that is, Abraham's literal, biological descendants) in various contexts, such as being promised the sacred land of Israel. On such a view, only the literal descendants should truly be called Jewish. Of course, as we have seen, such a view was dismissed by no less than Abraham himself, who "gathered souls." Obviously if Abraham understood God's promise to apply only to biological offspring, Abraham would not have sought converts. Those converts were his spiritual children.

These and other objections to welcoming converts cannot and should not simply be dismissed. Neither separately nor together, however, do they accumulate into an argument that repeals the covenantal obligation to offer Judaism and welcome converts.

That obligation, embedded in the foundational beliefs of Judaism, found expression in the actions and institutions of early Jewish life. It is to that historical adventure that we now turn.

Q. Why are converts good Jews?

Epstein. After the last very extended answer, I want to end this section briefly. Converts are good Jews because they came to Judaism by choice. I wonder how many born Jews, had they been born into another religion, would have chosen to become Jewish. Converts are good Jews because they provide great hope in Jewish life, that our religion is attractive enough to draw those looking for a spiritual home. That attractiveness should make those who doubt the value of a Jewish heritage take it more seriously and examine it more closely. Converts are good Jews because they remind us that Judaism is not just an accident of birth but a great spiritual path to ourselves, to other people, to nurturing the natural world, and, ultimately, to God.

12
Conversion in Jewish Thought

Q. Was conversion discussed in the Bible?

Epstein. In answering this question, we have to be careful with the use of words. The people we today call Jews were called *ivri*—Hebrews, Judeans, or Israelites. The ancient Israelites did not have a concept of religious conversion because the notion of a religion as separate from a nationality was incoherent. Therefore a person did not join a religion and so could not, in the sense we use the term, "convert" to Judaism. Indeed, the terms *Jews* and *Judaism* did not exist.

While there were no "conversions," many non-Israelites joined the community. They did this most frequently through marriage or acceptance of the beliefs and practices of the community. Abraham and his descendants "converted" many pagans and servants into their people.

After the Israelites were slaves in Egypt, after their exodus with the "mixed multitude," and the receiving of the Torah on Mount Sinai, the Israelites returned to the land of Israel. Once they returned, they absorbed many Gentiles, including those who lived in Canaan (such as the Hittites, Hivvites, Girgashites, Amorites, Perizzites, Jebusites, and others) and those who came as travelers into the land of Israel.

Some of these foreigners, the *nachri*, remained apart from the *ezrach*, the native Israelites. Some of the nachri decided to join the Israelites. When they did join, they were given a new social status. They became *gerim* (Hebrew for 'strangers'). A *ger* would be taken to the holy mountain and there make sacrifices so as to join the Israelites in a formal way.

Gerim often became part of the Israelites by marriage. For example, many pagan women who married Jewish men simply were absorbed into the men's clan, and they therefore accepted the clan's religious views. The marriages that resulted were seen as morally good because pagans would turn from idolatry to God through such marriages.

The gerim were permanent residents in the land of Israel, but they were not landowners. All gerim who joined a family or tribe were to be given equal rights and equal responsibilities, although the permission for them to participate in religious rituals developed over time.

The Israelites were told many times in the Torah to love the gerim, for the Israelites had been strangers in Egypt.

Indeed, there are numerous references to gerim in the Torah. In particular, the gerim were to be given equal responsibility, equal roots, to receive special consideration, they were not to be oppressed, and they were to be loved as Israelites loved themselves.

The prophets in the Bible had an enormous influence in understanding Israel's mission to the world in general and the role of conversion in that mission in particular. Amos was perhaps the first universalist. The prophet believed that God had entered into only one covenant at a time rather than entering simultaneous covenants. Also, Amos could not conceive of Israel worshipping God outside the land of Israel

Amos's famous disciple Isaiah (c. 740–700 B.C.E.) believed that Israel had to follow God's ethical teachings. This was a vital step in Jewish efforts to welcome converts, for a critical connection had been made. Isaiah concluded that if God is God of the whole world, not just Israel, and if God had revealed divine laws at Mount Sinai— so that the Israelites had specific ethical teachings to follow—then it follows that those laws and that requirement to follow ethical teachings apply not just to the Israelites but to all the people on earth. If the ethical rules applied to all, then Israel had a task: teach those ethical rules to humans.

The next step occurred when the prophet Jeremiah sent a letter to the Babylonian exiles telling them to pray for the welfare of their community as it existed in Babylon. By doing this, Jeremiah changed the views of Amos and Hosea, arguing that God could be worshipped outside the land of Israel. The God of Israel was to be available anywhere in the world.

Such an insight about God transformed not only the theological views of the Israelites, but their view of Gentiles living outside the Holy Land. Just as the concept of a "portable God" made it possible for Israelites to retain their identity outside their promised land, so, too, did such a concept of God allow for Gentiles living outside the land to join the people not by moving to the land of Israel, but by adopting the religious views of the Jews. The Gentiles, under this view, could join the Jewish people by worshipping God, by renouncing their pagan ways, and by accepting new beliefs. It was this central insight that made conversion to Judaism ultimately both possible and desirable. This final step took some time, but, at last, all the logical steps leading up to it were in place.

In foreign lands, of course, gerim could not join the Israelites in the same way as they had done in the land of Israel. This fact changed the basic idea of who a ger was. Converts were now termed nilvim, those who attached themselves to God (Isaiah 56:3,6; Esther 9:27; Zechariah 2:15; Isaiah 14:1) or nivdalim, people who left the non-Jewish world to follow the Holy Law (Ezra 6:21).

If worshipping God on foreign soil was possible for Israelites, and Gentiles could accept God anywhere, then it followed that worshipping God was possible for all humanity in every land. Only after Israel realized that God's laws and ethical teachings were meant for all humanity and that God could be worshipped by pagans everywhere (that is, without having to move to the land of Israel) could there arise the idea that the entire world could follow God's laws.

Armed with this insight, with Ezekiel's statement that God wished to be worshipped by all people, and with the already long-standing and powerful belief that idolatry was a sin, the Israelites needed only a few more steps before they could realize the moral need for proselytizing.

The next step was a belief that God would punish sins. It was crucial for the Israelites to believe that sin is not only wrong but results in punishments. Only with this belief could the Israelites feel the moral compulsion to confront idolaters in order to make them aware that they were sinning and might be punished for immoral behaviors.

It was Deutero-Isaiah (c. 540 B.C.E.) who provided the last necessary step for the Israelites to understand their mission. Deutero-Isaiah asked the question that emerged from all this theological development: Who would teach the Gentile nations about God, about divine truth? Who would make humanity follow the moral laws of the covenant? Who would save humanity from divine retribution by making them aware of wrongdoing? Who would, in Isaiah's insightful metaphor, free prisoners from (spiritual) imprisonment? The answer, of course, was that the people Israel were the divine teachers. The Israelites were charged with teaching the world about God.

God had revealed the moral truth to them, had given them the toughening discipline of exile, and would return the Jews to their land to become God's servants and become the moral teachers for all humanity; to become God's active witnesses to the world; to become, in Deutero-Isaiah's famous image, a light unto the nations. Israel was to bring God's revelation to the world and with it truth so that all humanity could be redeemed.

It was also Deutero-Isaiah who transformed the way Israel understood spiritual change from the assimilation of strangers in earlier times to the new idea of religious conversion, from a gradual, sometimes accidental process to a specific process with defined rituals. The Jewish concept of religious conversion is first clearly defined in Isaiah 56:1–8.

One fundamental implication of those insights was that Jews should offer their religion and welcome converts. They now had all the necessary theory.

It is therefore not in the least surprising that on Rosh Hashanah in 516 B.C.E., at the very moment that the Second Temple was being dedicated, Zechariah proclaimed such a program of seeking converts to Judaism (Zechariah 8: 20–23). This proselytizing program was undertaken for the next quarter century.

Eventually, a particularist reaction weakened the Jewish universalist movement, especially after the legislation mentioned in Ezekiel 44:6–9 was enacted in 458 B.C.E.

The return of Ezra in 458 B.C.E. and Nehemiah in 444 B.C.E. brought back the particularist strand of Jewish thought. This strand focused on the other legitimate view of Judaism—as a specific people who were apart from the world. Proselytism was halted. Opposition to this isolation was expressed in *Ruth* and *Jonah*, but the particularists won for three-quarters of a century as Jews regrouped and focused only on battling significant internal problems such as intermarriage.

Q. What about the Talmud? I've heard it has negative comments about converts.

Epstein. The Biblical terminology used to discuss the subject of conversion was redefined by the rabbis. For example, the rabbis understood a *ger* as referring specifically to a convert to Judaism and not just to a stranger. The rabbis made a distinction between two types of *gerim*. A *ger toshav*, or settler convert, also called a *ger ha-shaar* (or proselyte of the gate, as in Exodus 20:10), was a resident alien given permission to live in land controlled by Jews if he or she did not worship other gods or engage in idolatry of any kind or blaspheme God. The ger toshav agreed in the presence of three scholars to follow these Jewish principles. In addition, a ger toshav had to observe the Noachide Laws. The ger toshav did not perform work on the Sabbath, but was not required to join in worship or perform specifically Jewish religious commandments. Maimonides called them righteous Gentiles. They were clearly not full converts to Judaism.

The second category of gerim was the *ger tzedek*, a righteous convert, one who converted for the sake of religious truth and not for any other motive. (Such a ger was also called a *ger emet*, a true proselyte, or a *ger ben b'rit*, a proselyte who is a child of the covenant.) These gerim followed, not just the principles of Judaism, but also its rituals and practices. They are mentioned in the thirteenth blessing of the *Amidah*.

Some people, the *gerurim*, converted to Judaism for non-religious reasons such as marriage or a perceived economic or other advantage. Such proselytes (including, for example, the Gibeonites who became Jewish by a trick to avoid destruction and those who had been forcibly converted) were considered to be fully Jewish.

In addition to those who formally converted there was another group mentioned in Psalms and by Josephus, among other places. This group, known as "God-fearers," frequently kept the Sabbath and many believed in monotheism and prophetic ethics. They did not eat meat from a pig, but they did not observe the other prescribed rituals of Judaism.

They were not proselytes, just Gentiles following many Jewish customs in a very wide variety of ways. The God-fearers, sometimes called semi-proselytes, were said to include the magi of Persia, the Gymnosophists of India, and such well-known Greek thinkers as Plato, Aristotle, and many of the stoics.

Part of the problem with developing such categories is that, apart from those who formally converted, there were many ways with which Gentiles identified with Judaism short of actually becoming Jewish.

The destruction of the Second Temple in 70 c.e. and the defeat of Bar Kochba (135 c.e.) marked the end of a Jewish nation for almost 2,000 years. This loss of a nation made the Jewish people focus less on national matters and more on religion. The Jews themselves still had a favorable attitude toward converts, and Judaism was still considered attractive by many, but various factors imperiled efforts to win converts.

The external restrictions imposed on a stateless and militarily weak Jewish people by Christian and Muslim authorities were a major factor in the decline of proselytism.

Converts, for instance, were persecuted by Domitian between 81 and 96 C.E. The converts' property was confiscated, and they were sentenced to death or exile. In 131 C.E. Hadrian prohibited circumcision and public instruction in Judaism. Five years later he added to the list of prohibitions the observance of the Sabbath and the public performance of any Jewish ritual. In the year 200 the Emperor Severus promulgated laws forbidding heathens to embrace Judaism. In 325 Constantine reenacted Hadrian's law, forbidding Jews to convert slaves or engage in any proselytizing activity. In 330 Emperor Constantius decreed that Jews would forfeit any slaves converted to Judaism and the circumcision of a Christian slave carried a death penalty and the confiscation of property. Seven years later Constantius passed a law confiscating all property of a Christian who converted to Judaism. These and other early prohibitions greatly affected Jewish religious leaders.

The rabbis who wrote and edited the Mishnah and the Gemara, as well as other writings, had, as has been seen, generally favorable attitudes toward converts. Drawing on the prophetic implications that proselytism was, in effect, the Jewish mission, the rabbis saw conversion as affirming both the truth and the eventual triumph of Judaism.

These conversions did not stop even after the loss of national sovereignty. In the second and third centuries there continued to be a series of conversions, especially among the intellectuals. Both Raba and Rab Ashi, Babylonian scholars in the fourth century, vociferously advocated proselytism. It seems as though entire villages approached Rabbah ben Aboah to be converted, and the Talmud notes that Mahoza, a major Jewish community, had many proselytes (*Avodah Zarah* 64a: *Kiddushin* 73a).

The post-Mishnaic minor tractate *Gerim* detailed a procedure for welcoming converts; provided regulations regarding circumcision, ritual baths, and sacrifices, defined the *ger toshav*; and reminded the Jews that they were to have a friendly attitude toward converts.

There are negative comments in the Talmud about the Jewish people seeking converts, but they are relatively few and can be explained in historical context, as idiosyncratic to the individual making them, as reportorial. Rabbi Helbo, for example, said converts were "as difficult as a sore" because they caused Jews trouble. Another intrepretation of this most famous anti-conversion text is that converts were so diligent about keeping the commandments that they made born Jews upset.

Q. When did the tradition to discourage a convert three times come about? Is it still done?

Epstein. This idea was first mentioned in the Talmud. It was done, evidently for prudential reasons and to make sure that the convert was sincere. Some traditional rabbis still do it as a nod to this ancient idea, but most rabbis I know are very welcoming even from the outset. They see this tradition of discouraging conversion as tied to particular historic times when Jews were severely persecuted for welcoming converts. Now that those times are gone, Jews can go back to their original idea of being more welcoming.

Q. Where else in Jewish writing is conversion discussed?

Epstein. Conversion is included in various midrashim. Midrash is an examination of a Biblical text with an explanation about its meaning. There are many midrashic stories about converts. For example, in Exodus Rabbah 1:29, there is a story that prior to slaying the cruel Egyptain taskmaster (Exodus 2:12), Moses foresaw that there would be not a single convert from among the taskmaster posterity; it was this perception that justified the death.

In addition to many other kinds of literature, there is discussion about conversion in various responsa. Responsa were answers to questions of Jewish law given by authorities usually in response to a letter that posed the question. The great medieval thinker Maimonides wrote a famous letter to Obadiah the proselyte.

Indeed, Jewish literature is filled from its beginnings with positive references to converts.

13
Conversion in Jewish History

Q. Who were some famous converts?

Epstein. There are many well-known converts in Jewish history. In addition, there are a tremendous number who are not well-known but who made valuable contributions to their families and to the Jewish people. It is not possible to list even most of the well-known converts. Note that I have not included entertainers (such as Sammy Davis, Jr., Marilyn Monroe, Elizabeth Taylor, and many others) or sports figures. I've tried only to include those people who, in one way or another, contributed to Jewish life.

Abraham and Sarah were the founders of a people who would later be called the Jewish people. They left pagan beliefs in many gods and believed in one God. This revolutionary concept transformed the world. After coming to understand that there was one God, they went and "converted" others to their beliefs and away from pagan ideas. What is vital about Abraham and Sarah is that they were not the first people in the Bible. It is instructive that the Hebrew Bible does not have the first humans discover the truth about God, a crucial fact underscoring the notion that the founders of the Israelites were not born into an existing people. Thus, Abraham and Sarah are perfect models for humanity that can come to transform itself into believers in one God.

The story of the royal house of Adiabene is told by historian Josephus (and is repeated in the Talmud). A small kingdom on the Tigris River, its Crown Prince, Izates, the Queen Mother, and at least some if not all of its people were converted in the first century. Izates was converted by a merchant named Ananias, and his mother by another merchant named Hananya.

Reuel Abraham was born with the name Karl Heinz Schneider. He lived in Germany and helped to organize Hitler youth battalions. When Schneider turned 18, he volunteered to join the Luftwaffe and serve in combat. One day, he chanced to walk through a town in Poland, by then under Nazi occupation. Schneider saw storm troopers killing a group of Jews. They were all standing in the courtyard of a synagogue; the rabbi of the synagogue died while holding tightly onto the Torah. That experience changed the young Nazi. He began disobeying his orders. He pretended to be ill. He dropped bombs into lakes or parts of a forest that were uninhabited. He fixed detonators so that the bombs he dropped could not explode.

After World War II had ended, Schneider made a vow. He planned to be penitent for 20 years to atone for the sins he had committed. During those years he worked in coal mines and anonymously donated two-thirds of his wages to various agencies that aided both Jewish orphans of the war and those Jews who had survived the concentration camps. In addition, he taught himself Hebrew, bought a Bible that had been published in Israel, and began attending Sabbath services in a synagogue in Frankfurt.

After the 20 years were completed, he sold his land and bought a farm in Israel. Once he moved to Israel, he went to see rabbinical authorities in Haifa. His request was simple: he wished to convert to Judaism. The Supreme Religious Court of Israel investigated the amazing story he told, and he was ultimately accepted. He changed his name to Reuel Abraham and became a citizen of Israel.

Aquila (second century C.E.) was a translator of the Bible into Greek. He may have been a relative of Hadrian, a Roman Emperor.

Bodo-Eliezar (c. 893 C.E.) was a Roman Catholic archdeacon serving King Louis the Pious. He converted to Judaism and took the name Eliezar.

Bulan was the king of the Khazars. His story is told in the next question.

Abraham Isaac Carmel (born 1911) was named Kenneth Cox at birth. He was a priest who converted to Judaism. Having served as a priest for seven years, he eventually began to doubt his belief that Jesus was divine and searched around for a solution. He began to read the scholarly book *From Jesus to Paul* (New York: Macmillan, 1943) by Josef Klausner. One of Klausner's principal themes in the book was that Jesus was a simple Jewish "rabbi" whose Jewish teachings were transformed by Paul into a dogmatic system with a powerful organization. Carmel concluded that Paul, not Jesus, was the true founder of Christianity as we know it. Armed with this insight, Carmel reexamined his whole belief system. Eventually, he converted to Judaism, becoming a popular and much-admired educator. His moving story is told in his book *So Strange My Path* (New York: Bloch, 1993).

Warder Cresson (1798–1860) was declared insane after he converted to Judaism. His wife and children believed that, in nineteenth-century America, such a decision had to be a sign of insanity.

Previously Cresson was almost perpetually on a search for religious truth. Initially through a congressional connection, Cresson got an appointment as the first American consul to Jerusalem. Cresson lost the appointment but continued to Jerusalem with the aim of converting Jews to Christianity.

From 1844 until 1847 Cresson worked with the missionaries, but more and more Cresson began to identify with the Jews he met. By 1848 he decided to convert to Judaism. He took the name Michael C. Boaz Israel. He returned to Philadelphia in 1849, planning to settle his personal affairs and bring his family back to the land of Israel. Instead, his family had him declared insane and committed to an insane asylum. A court ruled him insane. Cresson appealed the verdict, and his trial, held in May 1851, went on for six days and was nationally covered. Cresson was declared sane. After the trial, Cresson divorced his wife, moved back to Israel, and remarried. When he died, he was buried on the Mount of Olives and all Jewish-owned businesses in Jerusalem were closed on the day of his funeral.

Favius Clemens (first century C.E.) was the nephew of the Roman Emperor Vespasian and a Roman consul.

Lord George Gordon (1757–93) was a member of the British House of Lords who became Jewish in 1787. He was later accused of libel against the government and died in prison.

Dahya al-Kahina (died in 698 or 702 C.E.) was the Berber warrior queen. Her tribe, the Jarawas, was in southeast Algeria about the time that the Arabs conquered North Africa. She and her whole tribe converted to Judaism and helped to block the Arab invasion for several years.

Ulrike Kohout was in the Stadttempel synagogue in Vienna on August 29, 1981. While there, the Palestine Liberation Organization attacked the synagogue. Kohout had converted two years earlier. She died in that attack while trying to shield the 2-year old son of one of her friends.

Abraham Kotsuji was born in Japan in 1899. Originally a follower of the Shinto religion, he converted to Christianity and was a specialist in the Hebrew language. During World War II, Kotsuji aided Jews who were escaping from the Nazis. He eventually decided to join the Jewish people and told his fascinating story in his book *From Tokyo to Jerusalem*.

Nahida Ruth Lazarus (1849–1928) was a German Christian. She married the philosopher Moritz Lazarus and wrote on many Jewish subjects later in her life.

Obadiah (late eleventh century—first half of twelfth century) was a priest born in Italy. Shortly after his ordination, he dreamed about converting to Judaism. He began to read the Hebrew Bible and to study the history of the Jews, and was especially moved by the persecutions that the Jews had suffered. In 1102 he converted to Judaism.

Onkelos Bart Kalonymus (second century c.e.), the nephew of the Emperor Titus, translated the Hebrew Bible into Aramaic.

Valentine Potocki (died 1749) was a Polish count. He saw a tavern owner studying the Talmud and became interested in Judaism. Eventually he converted, taking the name Abraham ben Abraham. He was praying one day in the synagogue. A young boy made some noise, and Potocki yelled at the boy for disturbing his praying. The boy's father was a powerful man and had Potocki arrested because he had abandoned Christianity, an act that was a crime. Rather than abandon his faith, Potocki was burned at the stake. A friend took Potocki's ashes and buried them in a Jewish cemetery. Eventually a tree grew over the spot, but Polish vandals eventually desecrated the gravesite.

Ruth (c. eleventh century b.c.e.) was the most famous convert in the Bible. I have told her story elsewhere, but I will just repeat here that when her Jewish husband died, Ruth did not abandon her mother-in-law, but became part of the Jewish people. As the great-grandmother of King David, and thus an ancestor of the Messiah in Jewish tradition, Ruth showed how crucial converts could be in Jewish history.

Sancheriv was the king of Assyria. Shmaya and Avtalyon, who taught Hillel and Shammai, were his descendants.

Sisra was a Roman army general. The great Rabbi Akiva was one of his descendants.

Catherine Weigel (c. 1460–1539) was a widow of a Jewish member of the municipal council in the city of Cracow. In 1530, Catherine Weigel, who had converted to Judaism, was arrested and accused of seeking to spread the message of Judaism to other people. She suffered martyrdom rather than give up her beliefs.

Q. Who were the Khazars?

Epstein. The Khazars were a Turkic people who lived between the Black and Caspian Seas in Southern Russia. The royal house of the Khazars converted to Judaism in the 720s and soon the whole

Khazar people did the same. Legend has it that King Bulan of the Khazars held a debate among speakers for Judaism, Islam, and Christianity. It was on the basis of that debate that the king chose to accept Judaism. It is more likely that instead of such a debate, Jewish traders, travelers, and refugees introduced Judaism to the Khazars. Eventually, the Khazaria kingdom fell. Evidently, some of its Jewish population went to Eastern Europe and the rest disappeared.

The most important influence of the Khazars was their effect on medieval Jews. It was a difficult era for the Jewish people, in which Christianity and Islam had not only risen but had conquered between them much of the world. Simultaneously, the Jews had lost their nation and political and military power.

Therefore, the conversion of a whole kingdom must have given the Jews a great sense of encouragement. Such a conversion illustrated for the Jewish community that Judaism was still attractive. It is no accident that Judah Halevi (c. 1075–1141) found the story of the Khazars a perfect starting point for explaining Judaism. Halevi's classic work *Sefer ha-Kuzari* sees in the act of conversion the essence of the Jewish message and the Jewish mission.

Q. Did Jews ever actually seek converts?

Epstein. There is much scholarly debate on this issue. It depends on what one means by "seeking." There were a variety of methods used that fall under the general term of Jewish proselytizing. Usually the term meant one of the following:

1. Judaism was "offered" to Gentiles not by engaging in specific activities but by waiting for God to bring the Gentiles to Judaism. This method was favored by those who believed solely in a passive mission.

2. Jews wrote and distributed literature that was specifically aimed at attracting potential converts. This literature was naturally secondary to such sacred literature as the Bible or Talmud. The missionary literature had the specific aim of telling those unfamil-

iar with Judaism about its moral beauty and, thus, to convince them of Judaism's attractiveness. Such literature included, among other works, the *Sibylline Oracles*, Josephus's *Contra Apionem*, Philo's *Apologia hyper Ioudaion* (a work no longer in existence), the *Letter of Aristeas*, *Joseph and Aseneth*, and material by Eupolemus, Demetrius, and Aristobulus. There is clear evidence that the *Septuagint*, the oldest Greek translation of the Bible, was prepared, in part, to offer Judaism to non-Jewish Greeks. In the translation *ger* was translated as 'proselyte'. The translator is believed to be Onkelos (Aquila), himself a proselyte. In particular, emphasis is placed on a Jewish missionary task in the translation of the Book of Isaiah.

3. The synagogue service was also used to offer Judaism to potential converts, but in an indirect fashion. The synagogue's principal function was to explain the Torah to Jews. In the non-Jewish sense of the word 'mission', the synagogue did not then engage in missionary work. However, the synagogue's very presence and mystery to many non-Jews combined its openness and hospitality to invited guests and visitors to make it an important place for potential converts to investigate Judaism. Those who had a natural curiosity about Judaism, that is, had a place to go. They were not always directly invited in; their own interest brought them to the synagogue's doors, and the Jewish notion of "offering" meant, in this case, making Judaism available by having public houses of worship and allowing non-Jews to enter. Of course, individual Jews no doubt invited friends to enter. Once inside the synagogue, visitors came into contact with the prayers and reading of the Torah. In the synagogue and elsewhere, non-Jews saw a religious and ethical system and a set of practices they admired, especially the Sabbath and the dietary laws, that stood in considerable contrast to the ways in which they had been reared. The Jewish alternative to pagan, Greek, or other beliefs was attractive to many, and they sought further instruction. There is a reference in Philo (*De Septinario*, 6) to "thousands of houses of instruction in all the towns," a reference that may be to the many synagogues functioning as learning centers for Gentiles.

4. There is conflicting evidence about whether or not there were ever any organized Jewish "missionaries." In general, however,

Judaism did not have a need to create a specific missionary occupation in the way it is commonly understood because, as the occasion warranted, all individual Jews would spread the religion. Just as all Jews felt themselves obligated to pray, so they felt obligated to share Judaism, to bring Gentiles under the wings of the Divine Presence. For example, it was an actor named Alityrus who interested Poppaea, the wife of Nero, in Judaism. That is, it is more accurate to talk of personal approaches made by Jews to non-Jews than of those by missionaries. The personal approaches were made in various ways, such as by inviting non-Jews to attend a synagogue, participate in a Jewish practice, listen to an exposition of Jewish thought, or read a piece of literature, when non-Jews expressed an interest in Judaism or asked a question or discussed religious or philosophical views. Because there were many Jews who were travelers and merchants, non-Jews frequently came into contact with Jewish practices and ideas on a regular basis. Some of the Gentiles asked questions about particular matters. Because the religious education Jews gave themselves and their children made virtually all Jews religiously knowledgeable and observant, even ordinary Jews could answer questions and provide living models of a Jewish way of life. The early literature lists large numbers of actual and probable converts, some famous, most not. Gentile merchants traveling through Judea, for example, frequently converted because they were attracted to the ethical way of life of the Jews.

Gentiles also approached Jews on a personal basis because the Gentiles were befriended by Jews or observed Jews performing good deeds, but Jews didn't, for instance, go out on the streets stopping strangers and seeking converts because such an act was considered pagan.

5. The education of Jews and especially of Jewish children extended to non-Jewish children who were adopted by Jews. If Philo is to be believed, the Jews regularly took in children who had been cast off by their Gentile families. Such children became Jews and were reared as Jews. Adoption of non-Jews may be seen as analogous to Judaism's earliest methods of offering Judaism to their

servants and to the non-Jewish resident aliens in their land or those living outside the land of Israel but among Jews. That is, many non-Jews who naturally lived among Jews and came in daily contact with Jewish religious activities were invited to participate in those activities.

6. Another way in which Jews actually welcomed converts, and thus a way that defined 'offering', was through marriage (*Yevamot* 92b). The marriage partners frequently converted to Judaism, and the children of intermarriages were raised as Jews. Interestingly, there were few objections to Jews marrying converts, at least until Christianity arrived to challenge Judaism.

Q. Why did Jews stop seeking converts?

Epstein. Slowly, over time, the Rabbinic attitude, and the Jewish people's attitude, changed from one of actively welcoming converts to one of discouraging those who wished to convert. This incredible, basic transformation took place over several centuries and had a series of causes.

Christianity's rise was a vital factor in ending Jewish efforts to welcome converts. Christianity used the Jewish missionary zeal and methods, ultimately transforming the Jewish concept of conversion from an ideal (that is, Judaism was to be offered but was not required for salvation) into a requirement (that is, a person could not be saved without converting to Christianity) and transforming the means of effecting conversion from offering by the means described above into intrusive missionary work with intense emotional and later physical pressure to convert.

When such zeal was combined with a relaxation by Paul of existing conversionary obligations, especially circumcision, the Christians became very successful in attracting converts. Indeed, many Gentiles close to Judaism, who had not formally converted, chose instead to take the easier route and become Christians. The rabbis began to discourage would-be converts for fear that instead of becoming Jewish they would become Christian.

Another reason for the change was that the horrible defeats by the Romans had turned Jewish life inward, making it focus on religion and ritual observance rather than nationalism and militarism as a means of survival. The inwardness did not result in just a transformation from nationalism to religious preoccupation, but also from a concern about the non-Jewish world to a focus on the Jewish one. The rabbis saw their mission increasingly as one of educating Jews about the Torah and making them follow religious laws. This mission, in brief, was one of survival; saving the world couldn't take place while the Jews first had to save themselves. The rabbis were trapped and desperate. They had to preserve Judaism under the most trying circumstances but still felt the missionary obligation to welcome Gentiles. The rabbis praised conversion, going so far as to put the praise in daily Jewish prayer. But fear of persecution and the need for self-preservation in the Diaspora was making the Jews a religious body segregated from the Gentiles by both external legal authority and internal religious authority. If seeking converts would endanger the very existence of the Jewish community, the Jewish leaders would take the prudential route of protecting the community. If the Godly mission was not to be allowed by contemporary history, Rabbinic Judaism organized to protect and preserve the Jewish people for the day when that mission could be resumed.

Q. When did Jews begin seeking converts again?

Epstein. The Jewish people did not redevelop an ideology that included actively encouraging converts until the new Reform movement developed the idea in a new guise in the nineteenth century. The founding thinkers of the Reform movement were operating in a post-Enlightenment world. They rejected traditional Jewish law and asserted that Judaism's attractiveness would be enhanced if it embraced universally accepted moral values as its core and presented itself to the world in a fashion that would be familiar and therefore comfortable to non-Jews. The particularist elements of Judaism were deemphasized. Jewish nationalism was declared as being at odds with Jews acting as full citizens in the countries in which they lived. Selected universal moral teachings of Judaism, most specifically as embodied in the Prophets, were advanced as the heart and soul of Judaism.

This was, of course, a liberal universalism and not a Jewish universalism. Had their universalist ideas been more grounded in Jewish roots, and more sociologically sophisticated about the elements needed for any such mission's success, those Reform thinkers would have maintained attachment to Jewish law even if reinterpreting it, embraced Jewish nationalism, and kept the particularist ceremonies.

In advancing their view, though, the Reform thinkers reintroduced into theological discourse the very concept of universalism in Jewish life, however conceived.

Similarly, in suggesting that Judaism contained the moral values that all people could embrace, these reformers were led to another great historical contribution: the reintroduction of the concept of historical mission in Jewish life. Reform Jewish thinkers secularized the messianic interpretations of the original Jewish mission. In rejecting chosenness, these thinkers replaced it with the notion that each people on earth has a mission and the Jews' mission was a religious one to advance the social conditions of humanity by making people adhere to the ideals of classical prophetic Judaism. Reform Jews saw their new Judaism as fully capable of being acceptable to the entire world while simultaneously saving that world.

The problem for these Reformers was that their idea of mission was not so much to bring Gentiles to traditional Judaism as it was to bring Gentiles to an already accepted liberal ethical system conceived of as identical to normative Judaism.

This inaccurate understanding of the Jewish mission explains why Gentiles did not become Jewish. Even liberal Gentiles friendly to Jews already accepted those moral principles and were already willing to fight for the same social goals as were Reform Jews. These liberal Gentiles saw no need to call themselves by the name "Jewish." Liberal Gentiles were not offered the particularist elements of Judaism along with the universal and so, naturally, they saw no substantive distinction between Judaism and their own religion. They therefore not only did not convert but did not even see Judaism as a distinctive alternative to consider.

The misinterpretation of the Jewish mission by the early Reformers was important because their misinterpretations became the standard modern definitions of those concepts. This led to significant mistakes, such as the identification of "universalism" in Jewish life with liberal universalism rather than with a more specifically Jewish universalism, the identification of "mission" with the Reformist notion rather than the Jewish universalist notion, and the inaccurate identification of Jewish nationalism as antithetical to the Jewish mission to be a light unto the nations.

Despite these misinterpretations, the Reform movement had made an extraordinary contribution to the reclamation of the Jewish obligation to welcome converts.

The Reform movement made its greatest headway in the United States, where there had always been conversion to Judaism. Many of the early converts were African slaves, some of whose descendants formed Jewish congregations.

American Jewry was changed after the 1848 revolution in Germany failed, bringing religiously liberal refugees to the United States. Some of the children of these refugees married Jews and wished to convert. Their fascinating stories were carefully traced in several Jewish periodicals such as *The Occident* (1843–69) and *The American Israelite* (founded in 1854).

Various American Reform rabbis emphasized conversion in their theology. Rabbi David Einhorn (1809–79) so regularly admitted converts to his congregation, Har Sinai in Baltimore, that his prayer book included a specific service to accept converts. Einhorn fervently believed that Judaism would become universally accepted.

Isaac Mayer Wise (1819–1900), who founded the central institutions of Reform Judaism in the United States, noted with satisfaction the increase in converts. On November 3rd to 6th, 1869, Reform rabbis held a conference in Philadelphia, reaffirming that the purpose of their exile was "to lead the nations to the true knowledge and worship of God." At the 1885 Pittsburgh Conference the Reform rabbis recognized the Bible as the "consecration of the Jewish people to its mission as the priest of the One God."

Other Reform leaders who supported the mission concept included Kaufmann Kohler, Samuel Schulman, and Leo Baeck. Baeck (1873–1956) wrote in his famous book *The Essence of Judaism* (New York: Schocken, 1948) that "the Jewish religion is intended to become the religion of the whole world . . . Every presupposition and every aim of Judaism is directed towards the conversion of the world to itself."

As the Reform movement began to affect the way conversion was seen, the other two large American Jewish religious movements also were evolving their views on proselytizing.

The Orthodox movement was split on this issue at the end of the nineteenth century. One part of the movement permitted conversions of those whose motives included marriage to Jews and encouraged Jews to accept the conversion of children of Jewish fathers and Gentile mothers to Judaism. This group consisted of such rabbis as Zvi Hirsch Kalishcher (also famous as a forerunner of Zionism), David Hoffmann, Marcus Horovitz, and the *Imrei David*, David Horowitz.

Another group of Orthodox rabbis was more stringent regarding conversion. This view prevailed after World War II for a variety of reasons. Intermarriage had greatly increased, emphasizing to the stringent a continuing need for Jewish self-segregation so that Jews and Gentiles could not meet and fall in love. Such self-segregation necessitated a decline in all interactions with Christians, including interactions that could lead to conversion to Judaism. Also, the Conservative and Reform movements had continued to grow and promote policies that the Orthodox often found troubling. The Orthodox reaction against leniency in conversion can to some extent be seen as a reaction especially to the Reform movement. By being strict, the Orthodox presented themselves as refusing to have the same pro-conversionary views that were widely identified with the Reform movement. Indeed, more and more, as Orthodoxy dismissed the religious legitimacy of the non-

Orthodox, the moderating influences within halachic discussions that once prevailed disappeared.

Conservative Jewry has always maintained balance between particularism and universalism within Jewish tradition. However, perhaps wary because the ideas of universalism and mission were reintroduced to the Jewish theological vocabulary by the Reform movement, Conservative Judaism has been reluctant to accept the missionary implications of the universalist strain in Jewish thought.

The Conservative movement has welcomed converts as a means to combat intermarriage, but not as a means to perform a specific covenantal mission. In part this is also because Conservativism is a pragmatic movement rather than an ideological one, focusing on solutions to the problems of Jewish life rather than on defining a specifically Conservative world view from which its views could be deduced. In part this is so because Conservative Judaism emerged as a reaction to Reform Judaism rather than from a definite ideology. Conservatives saw themselves confronting a pragmatic, not a theological, problem: how to keep tradition but make modifications to fit the tradition to modernity. Because of this it did not develop an ideology, but instead focused on what it perceived to be the central aspects of the Jewish tradition that cohered with modernity. Conservative Judaism saw Judaism as its ideology, so it sought no further clarification. Additionally, Conservatives have been concerned, with some historical justification, that a clearly articulated ideology would do more to divide than to unite those who call themselves Conservative Jews. In religious life, the Conservatives have often seen themselves as a middle course between Orthodoxy and Reform, judiciously steering their movement through the turbulent waters of American modernity. Such efforts require reacting to specific problems rather than operating out of a general ideology. Such an existential approach to life, however useful, leaves an ideological void, a void Conservatives only recently have come to recognize as limiting. Conservatives see that both Orthodoxy and Reform have much more clearly stated views, and the clarity has helped them.

There were individual voices in Conservative Jewry promoting conversion. Dr. Solomon Goldman, in his 1938 experimental prayerbook, wrote: "Judaism means to convert the world, not to convert itself . . . It hopes and prays and waits patiently for the Great Day when the world will be ripe for its acceptance."

Robert Gordis also focused on conversion in several writings, but most explicitly in a 1958 article in the *National Jewish Monthly* (March, 1958: 6-7; 24-27) forthrightly titled "Has the Time Arrived for Jewish Missionaries?" In the article, Dr. Gordis advocated a pilot missionary program for Japan and the establishment of Jewish information centers in the United States.

Despite various pro-conversionary views, none of the three major religious groups in the United States had ever embarked on a formal conversionary program. There were relatively few conversions and only a few, small conversionary efforts.

Such conversionary efforts were at first undertaken by small organizations favoring conversion, groups that began to arise after the Holocaust and the birth of Israel. (These groups included the United Israel World Union, the Jewish Information Society, and the National Jewish Information Service, among others.) Individual rabbis and authors praised conversion, but it was not an idea that was very valued in the Jewish community or very acceptable to any of its leaders.

By the late 1970s, however, much had changed in American Jewish life. The overt anti-Semitism in America had radically declined. There was a widespread perception among Gentiles that Judaism was a religion that emphasized family values, education, a tolerance toward those with differing religious views, personal morality, the social good, and a spiritual outlook on life. Jews were seen as model American citizens—and absolutely wonderful marriage partners. The changing attitude toward Jews by Gentiles and the continuing cultural assimilation by Jews into Gentile society led to a rapid increase in intermarriage. This increase caused alarm within the Jewish community, but also resulted in an unexpected development. In the late 1970s and early 1980s, between 30 and 40 percent of those marriage partners not born Jewish were converting to Judaism. The fear of intermarriage and the unexpected rise in voluntary conversions began to change attitudes.

At first, the rise in conversions that followed the rapid increase in intermarriages over the last 30 years was simply a surprise to many Jews. It had always been an unspoken assumption, both among Jewish leaders and in the general Jewish community, that intermarriage inevitably meant the loss of the Jewish partner to Jewish life. Jews had concluded that a principal reason for intermarriage was to escape the purported burdens of a Jewish identity. They were unsure about what to make of the many Jews who intermarried but wished to remain Jewish, not to mention those born Christian who chose to become Jews.

Yet Jews were pleased by such conversions at an elemental level. Seeing people who were born Gentile choose to become Jews validated the choice of those born Jewish to remain as Jews. The enormous step of conversion made the smaller step of remaining Jewish both easier and more sensible.

Just as has the rebirth of Israel, converts to Judaism provide American-born Jews with a sense of personal legitimacy. That this is so reflects, in part, the peculiar nature of American Jewry; its own fundamental character is voluntary. In a sense all American Jews are Jews by choice; people who are born Jews must choose to remain active Jews by such actions as choosing a marital partner, joining a synagogue or Jewish organization, and making other similar choices. There are no legal, and weakened religious, familial, and cultural forces that seek, reward, and support such a voluntary choice to remain a Jew. Thus the unique conditions of contemporary American Jewish culture have contributed to making born Jews appreciate the validation of their religious lives by Jews by Choice.

There are other aspects of the general religious culture of America that have also contributed to a climate in which Jews by choice would be welcome by Jews by birth. The rise of ethnicity as a socially approved organizing principle for defining identity has made Jews more willing to identify themselves and be identified in the society as Jews. The self-confidence that has emerged from this ethnic identification, which was dramatically supplemented by a pride that emerged from an identification with the efforts of the

people of Israel, has allowed American Jews to feel more comfortable in America, to put the American anti-Semitism of the 1920s,
1930s, and 1940s behind them, and even, to use a commercial
metaphor uniquely applicable to America, to place their product
up for sale alongside the other religious products already available
in the marketplace of religious ideas.

Additionally, an important part of the contemporary American
religious scene has been the visibility of cult groups and Evangeli-
cal ministers popular in the American media. The religious fervor
of both the cults and the Evangelicals was complemented by their
open desire to convert others to their beliefs and way of life. Their
beliefs and activities increased the legitimacy of conversion in
American culture, including conversion to Judaism. In addition,
the cultic and Christian efforts prompted a defensive response
against their conversionary overtures in the Jewish community. The
increase in acceptance of conversion can in this sense in part be
seen as an ironic acceptance of the aim (but not the tactics) of those
whom Jewish leaders saw as posing a religious threat; welcoming
converts became a way of fighting religious fire with religious fire.

Beyond these and other social and internal communal reasons,
the attitude of American Jews has been changed by the converts
themselves. They have spoken out in forums, on television, in
books, in synagogues, and in uncountable conversations, arguments, fights, and tear-filled pleas. They have requested acceptance,
and have frequently gotten it.

Sensing the changing attitudes, Rabbi Alexander Schindler, then
President of the Union of American Hebrew Congregations, a Reform group, delivered an address in December, 1978 to the Board
of Trustees of that organization, urging it to establish an outreach
program for the "unchurched," that is, those without formal religious affiliation. He proposed that Jews should try to attract non-
Jews to Judaism, especially the non-Jewish partners in intermarriages. The outreach program was intended to be unobtrusive,
taking the form of establishing information centers, educational
courses, and publications rather than such methods as door-to-
door missionary work. Rabbi Schindler's revolutionary point was

that Jews should not wait for potential or actual partners in an intermarriage to consider converting, but rather Jews should approach such partners about that possibility. Schindler wanted his movement to do the seeking, to identify and nurture those who might convert and support those who did. He sought to minimize Christian opposition to his proposal by ruling out seeking converts from among those who were already affiliated with another religion. The UAHC's Board of Trustees unanimously adopted Schindler's resolution and endorsed a Joint Task Force created along with the Central Conference of American Rabbis.

The Task Force presented its report to the 1981 UAHC General Assembly. That Assembly adopted five resolutions establishing an outreach program. In 1983, the Task Force was reformed as a Joint UAHC/CCAR Commission on Reform Jewish Outreach and was charged with, among other tasks, developing appropriate programs and visual materials for its various outreach audiences. The Commission has Regional Outreach Coordinators and has produced an impressive array of publications on the place of converts within Reform Judaism.

Other religious movements in America were also reacting to the changing times. In 1979, the Reconstructionist movement developed formal Guidelines on Conversion, including an outreach program. Their program was aimed directly at those who had already converted in order to help them integrate into the community.

The Conservative Movement eschewed the original mission idea inherent in Rabbi Schindler's approach, but nevertheless saw the value of preventing intermarriages by encouraging intermarried non-Jews to convert and making Judaism available (as opposed to intrusive proselytizing) to those who were interested. In 1985, the movement's Rabbinical Assembly approved a statement viewing the increase in conversions as a "positive" aspect of Jewish life, both as a reaction to intermarriage and as a personal religious quest. In 1987, the movement held its first Conference on Intermarriage and Conversion and was planning a common syllabus to use in teaching potential converts as well as other related efforts. Also in that year, the Rabbinical Assembly published *Embracing Judaism* (New

York: Rabbinical Assembly, 1987) by Simcha Kling, a book explaining Judaism that was especially aimed at potential converts. The Rabbinical Assembly also established Regional Conversion Institutes that provide introductory courses in Judaism that may lead students to convert, and the Assembly's Committee on *Keruv* and Giyur issued a *Keruv Resource Guide* in 1991. The United Synagogue of Conservative Judaism established a Committee on Intermarriage in 1991. By 1995, these committees joined in a Rabbinical Assembly–United Synagogue of Conservative Judaism Joint Commission on Responding to Intermarriage, with an active subcommittee that deals with issues involving conversion to Judaism.

The Orthodox movement continues to accept converts in principle, but to reject converts not converted according to what the Orthodox understand to be halachic standards. By their definition, no non-Orthodox conversion can be religiously valid because non-Orthodox rabbis are unqualified to serve as religious witnesses and because, according to many Orthodox, the formal conversion requirements and practices of the non-Orthodox don't conform to traditional Jewish law. Of course, non-Orthodox rabbis forcefully disagree with such a viewpoint.

There were other signs that the Jewish community was starting to welcome converts. Numerous programs and support groups organized by YM-YWHAs and Jewish Community Centers were established.

Despite the increase in efforts to welcome converts, two negative factors stand out. Firstly, none of the organized Jewish religious groups in the United States has yet explicitly revived the ancient idea of a covenantal mission to offer Judaism and welcome converts. Secondly, the percentage of conversions among the intermarrying or intermarried has declined. The reasons for this decline are varied and include a greater tolerance for intermarriage by American Jews and a greater willingness by rabbis to perform intermarriages without conversion. Some in the Jewish community also cite as a reason for the decline the Reform movement's patrilineality principle, which presumes that a child of a Jewish father and non-Jewish mother who identifies as a Jew is, in fact,

Jewish. This principle, at odds with Judaism's traditional matrilineal principle, has, it is claimed, reduced the urgency to get non-Jewish mothers to convert. Defenders of the principle say the very absence of pressure to convert leads not only to more converts but to converts who are more knowledgeable about and committed to Jewish life.

Q. What is the future of conversion to Judaism?

Epstein. I think the future for welcoming converts is going to be remarkable. There is going to be an ever-increasing acceptance of welcoming converts by the born-Jewish community and, I believe, a recognition that such efforts are not just prudential but at the heart of the Jewish enterprise in history. I also believe that more Gentiles will find Judaism an attractive alternative to the chaos of much of modern life. They will find its prayers as the original form of relaxation, its beliefs as sound and profound, its practices to be meaningful.

14

How to Welcome Converts to Judaism

Q. What can I do to welcome converts to Judaism?

Epstein. The "I" in this question will include all members of the Jewish community. Whether you are in a synagogue community, a Jewish Community Center, or elsewhere, you have a lot you can do. Let us consider how each aspect of the Jewish community can contribute to welcoming converts.

Welcoming converts to Judaism is important in contemporary Jewish life. One aspect of this importance is conversion's role in reducing the number of intermarriages. There are close to 200,000 people in the United States who have converted to Judaism. However, the percentage of conversions that would prevent or end an intermarriage has declined over the past several decades so that only a very small percentage of intermarriages concludes with a conversion.

Conversion to Judaism is a useful goal because it provides outreach with communally acceptable borders for its programs and connects outreach to prevention. While a significant number of intermarried couples are not immediately ready to discuss conversion, having conversion as a goal defines the sorts of programs in which outreach programs should engage, even if those programs bring a person very slowly toward a decision to consider conversion.

Some people oppose outreach to welcome converts, thinking the Jewish community should spend its time, energies, and money on preventing those who are already Jewish from intermarrying. However, there is a connection between welcoming converts and prevention.

What, then, can be done within the Jewish community to increase the number of conversions to Judaism? There is much to do for every institution in Jewish life.

Synagogues can establish *keruv* ('drawing in'), or outreach committees, to welcome, educate, integrate, and support people who wish to convert to Judaism. Synagogues can also offer adult education Introduction to Judaism courses, include discussions of conversion in the religious school curriculum, have pertinent articles in internal publications, have programs on conversion, establish a section in the library and Judaica shop of books and materials on and for converts, and, crucially, make these efforts widely known in the community.

Rabbis can give sermons and talks on conversion and help the *keruv* or outreach committee. Rabbinic seminaries can establish curricula and train future rabbis to welcome converts. Rabbinic groups can seek funds to hire rabbis to work full-time on conversion to Judaism in their particular regions.

Federations can fund local conversion programs.

Jewish Community Centers and Y's can continue to expand their educational efforts aimed at the intermarried, with material about conversion given a more prominent role at some stage in the education process. They can hire rabbis to give lectures on conversion or run Introduction to Judaism classes.

The Jewish media can run articles and stories about conversion. Jewish family service agencies can expand their efforts to have materials about conversion available and help to distribute such materials.

Jewish schools can incorporate material about conversion into their curricula.

Those who are part of an intermarried family can gently raise the subject of conversion and encourage any interest.

There is now a central, transdenominational effort to increase conversion. The Conversion to Judaism Resource Center (74 Hauppauge Road, Room 53, Commack, NY 11725, 516-462-5826) has been established to make the opportunity of conversion more widely known. The Center publishes pamphlets on conversion, places conversion materials in public, university, and synagogue libraries, maintains the Conversion to Judaism Home Page on the World Wide Web, puts would-be converts in touch with rabbis, places advertisements about conversion, and in general publicizes the option of conversion to Judaism.

If the Jewish community takes these steps the number of conversions to Judaism will dramatically increase. This will result in more Jews, more Jewish families, and a more stable Jewish communal life.

Q. How can I start a *keruv* ('outreach') committee?

Epstein. One significant contribution congregations can make to attract, train, and welcome converts to Judaism is to have a *keruv*, or outreach committee. *Keruv* is a Hebrew word meaning to 'draw in'. *Keruv* seeks to draw interested people to Judaism without changing Jewish standards. *Keruv* is used here instead of the word "outreach" because reaching out may be interpreted as modifying Judaism in order to attract outsiders, whereas *keruv* clearly means that Judaism remains the same as it welcomes those who wish to join it. Obviously individual committees can choose the name that they believe best suits them. For the purposes of this material, the terms are interchangeable.

Keruv, or outreach, is meant not only for unconverted Gentile partners in an intermarriage, but also for others, such as those who have already converted, and for all those with a spiritual interest in Judaism. Interestingly, many born Jews benefit greatly from *keruv* because, as they welcome non-Jews, they learn more about their own Judaism.

A congregational *keruv* committee can have several purposes. It can: (1) be a support group for converts; (2) help to integrate new converts into the congregational community; (3) serve as a source of information about conversion to Judaism for those in the congregation who are intermarried and are not Jewish; and (4) develop educational programs about Judaism and conversion for the congregation and the wider community. There are, of course, many other possible purposes.

A *keruv* committee needs someone to initiate it, either a rabbi, a congregational leader, or a congregant. That person needs to meet with the rabbi and other interested people. The rabbi's support is, of course, vital.

If you wish to organize such a committee at your congregation, talk with all the leaders of the congregation to seek ideas and approval. Then simply ask various people about who might be interested in such a committee. Use word-of-mouth to find five or six people. Call these people and ask if they would be interested in attending a meeting with the rabbi and other needed people.

The first meeting is important. It is vital to determine the specific purpose and structure of the group. Of course, a group can have several interrelated purposes. It is useful to have either one leader or a rotating leadership. It is also important to determine the eligibility for membership in the group. For example, you might decide that your group will be open to converts, their spouses, born Jews interested in the subject, and even anyone outside the congregation who wishes to learn about conversion or discuss it. (Obviously, this is a way ultimately to attract new members.)

A *keruv* committee can undertake a variety of projects depending on the interests and goals of the group. Many activities can be free or low cost. That is, *keruv* need not take monies from other vital programs within the synagogue. It is also a good idea to start with only one project, carry it through, evaluate it, and learn from it.

It is also crucial that a *keruv* committee's members be clear in their own feelings about the importance of conversion and express this view publicly when they discuss *keruv*.

There are many possible activities for a *keruv* group. Here are some of them:

1. Simply meet and discuss the experiences, joys, and difficulties of conversion, such as relations with parents, children, and the born Jewish community. Telling and hearing stories is helpful and fascinating.
2. Discuss those experiences in a public forum. You can send out news releases to newspapers and cable tv stations, which may print and broadcast notice of the meeting free. You can also decide to place advertisements in a local newspaper.
3. Have lectures by a group member with a special story, or bring in an outside lecturer on the subject.
4. Establish a *keruv* center in the library, with books and articles on the subject. If your synagogue sells books, have some titles on conversion available.
5. Meet with the synagogue staff regarding responding to questions about conversion.
6. Write articles about the group for the synagogue bulletin.
7. Support or establish an Introduction to Judaism program aimed at Gentiles who wish to learn about Judaism and explore the possibility of conversion.
8. Establish a host family program for new converts. In such a program, synagogue members show new Jews how to live Jewishly. Some areas of help might be in prayer, keeping a kosher home, keeping Shabbat, cooking, preparing a seder, and so on.
9. Work within the congregation to provide congregational members with reliable information about conversion. Ask the rabbi to include discussion of conversion in a sermon. Plan and hold public conversion ceremonies for those who wish it. Meet with students in the congregational school to discuss conversion and answer questions about it. Ask congregational men's and women's organizations to hold meetings on the subject.

10. Develop a package of materials for Gentiles who ask about conversion to Judaism.

Keruv committees in each congregation would enrich and strengthen Jewish life.

Q. How do I help publicize a conversion class?

Epstein. This section is intended to provide information on publicity for a conversion class aimed primarily or partially at potential converts to Judaism. The information is appropriate for conversion classes, Introduction to Judaism classes, and other similar programs, such as workshops or discussions on conversion to Judaism.

Publicity starts with the designation of one person to be in charge of publicity for the class. This person can be a rabbi, executive director of a congregation, an outreach or education director, or an interested congregant. The publicity director's job is to coordinate all publicity efforts with the help of as many other volunteers as possible. Here is a sample publicity schedule that can be adapted to meet local needs. It will be useful to have a Publicity Notebook to keep track of all efforts.

Twelve Weeks before the Class:

1. *Gather Together All Pertinent Information about the Class.*

All the basic information about the conversion class needs to be determined or decided. Such information includes, for example: (a) the nature of the course of study and the intended audience (for example, is it just for potential converts, or does it include or require the potential convert's romantic partner to attend? Is it available for born Jews? For anyone in the community?); (b) the location or locations of the class (for example, in a Jewish congregation, Jewish Community Center, or some other similar institution); (c) the number of sessions and their dates and times; (d) the subject matter or curriculum, texts, and other materials; (e) the instructors; (f) the cost and whether or not there are any scholarships available; (g) any special attractions about the course such as outside speakers or interesting hands-on experiences during the class; (h) the flexibility of the course, that is, can a student who misses a class make it up? Can students begin at various times or must they start at the beginning of the course? Are tutors available in person, or through phone, fax, or e-mail?; and (i) a contact name, address, and phone number for those seeking additional information.

2. Develop Your Mailing and Contact List.

Publicity starts with good information about local media and other contacts. Draw up a mailing and contact list of all key local people such as rabbis, Jewish educators, and editors or religious writers in Jewish and secular local papers. Those secular local papers should include standard newspapers plus such publications as college newspapers, local shopping papers, publications aimed at parents of young children, city magazines, and so on. In addition, the mailing list should include other local Jewish congregations within the movement of the congregation offering the conversion class; Jewish schools, including day schools; and organizations, such as Federations and Jewish Community Councils, Jewish Community Centers, local interested Jewish educational organizations, and Hillels; kosher food establishments such as butcher shops, delicatessens, and bagel stores; mohelim; radio and television stations; local bureaus of wire services; weekly entertainment guides; libraries, museums, colleges, and other educational places. For each name or place on the list, have an address, telephone number, and contact person, if known. Canvassing people for media contacts can be especially useful.

3. Gather Information about Other Conversion Classes, Publicity, and Advertising.

All examples of successful programs can be helpful. Contact the appropriate movement in Judaism for suggestions. In addition, contact other congregations and institutions that have run conversion classes or Introduction to Judaism programs and ask for sample news releases, flyers, and any other publicity materials they can show you. This is a good time to ask if there are any people in the organization who have a publicity or advertising background. Read about publicity and advertising.

4. Formulate a Publicity Schedule and Budget.

The suggestions in this pamphlet can be done at no cost or extremely low cost. Leave as much lead time as possible for publicity. The schedule should include as many of the suggestions listed below as possible.

5. Check with Media and Organizations on Your Mailing List about Their Deadlines.

Make a list of all the deadlines on a master publicity calendar and plan to send materials to them before those dates. Ask appropriate congregations and organizations if they will distribute flyers announcing the course, and if so, plan to send them flyers as well.

Eight Weeks before the Class:

6. Begin by publicizing within your congregation or organization.

Prepare a brief notice for the bulletin. Send a flyer to people who have taken conversion classes and who might have friends who are interested and to all members, or selected members, such as parents of students in the congregational school. Obviously if there is an outreach coordinator or group in the congregation, they should be included in seeking publicity for the class. Put posters up on bulletin boards. If possible, notices should appear in the bulletin several times as well as in any mid-month mailings.

7. *Write a news release.*

When it comes to letting those outside your congregation or organization know about the class, the heart of free publicity is the news release. Here are the steps to writing a press release:

A. Gather together all the information about the class as discussed above.

B. Use either congregational or organizational letterhead stationery or take a white 8½ x 11 piece of paper and type the name and address of the sponsoring organization in the upper left corner.

C. Below the name and address of the sponsoring organization, type: For further information, contact: and give the director of publicity's name and phone number (either at the organization or at home, preferably both).

D. Below that, type, in capital letters, FOR IMMEDIATE RELEASE, which means that the information can be printed or used immediately. If the information should be held for a specific date, type FOR RELEASE ON (date).

E. Next, in the center of the paper, capitalized, write a headline. Imagine your target audience reading a paper. Consider what would attract them.

F. Double-space your press release and use wide margins. Type it on one side of the page only, and limit the release to several paragraphs if possible. At most, the release should not be more than one page. If, for some reason, you must go on to another page—for example because you were asked to send a schedule of all classes—type "-more-" on the bottom of the first page and end the first page with a complete paragraph. The second page should contain an abbreviation of

your headline and a numbering of the page. At the conclusion of the press release type "end."

G. Indent the first paragraph. Provide in this paragraph a summary of the basic information about the course. A second
paragraph might include additional information, a quotation
from, for example, a rabbi teaching the course, or other related materials. Make sure you include information about
how those who are interested can get information about the
class.

H. Once the news release is finished and polished, it should be
shown to any appropriate rabbis, instructors, or committees
for final approval.

8.   Prepare Public Service Announcements (PSAs).

Public Service Announcements (PSAs) are timed messages for radio and television broadcast often made available for messages
deemed to be in the public interest and provided by tax-exempt
organizations. Some PSAs are videotaped or audiotaped, but these
can be very expensive. One much easier approach is to provide a
PSA script for announcers to read or put on the screen. There are
several steps needed to preparing a good PSA: (1) listen to local
radio and tv stations that provide PSAs to get a sense of their style
and what they want; (2) call the station to get the name of the public
affairs or public service director and what they require for a PSA,
such as a copy of the 501 (c) (3) tax exempt certificate; (3) prepare
four separate scripts for radio stations. These should be scripts for
10 seconds (10 to 15 words), 20 seconds (35 to 40 words), 30
seconds (55 to 65 words), and 60 seconds (120 to 125 words).
The scripts should be sent in using this form: a headline in capital
letters, the words "Public Service Announcement" on the next line,
and the length of the script—such as :60 Radio for a 60-second
radio spot—on the next line. This should be followed by the script
all in capital letters and with ellipses (. . .) whenever there should
be a pause. The language should be simple and direct. Always in-

clude a contact name and number. When you are finished, read the spot aloud and time it with a stopwatch.

If the PSA is to be put on the screen of a cable station, you can use the format employed in the flyer described below.

9. Prepare advertisements.

Paid advertising can also be very expensive. If your budget allows for it, keep these ideas in mind. One-shot ads rarely work. The principle of repetition is important in advertising, and therefore an effective advertising campaign is likely to be expensive. Quality is also crucial. If at all possible, ask someone with an advertising background or ask an ad agency to volunteer their efforts. In general, ads should have a strong headline. The most effective ads appear in the front section on the right-hand page and above the fold. Again, include a contact name, address, and phone number. Advertisements can be placed in a variety of publications. For example, if you have regular conversion classes, consider advertising in the local Yellow Pages.

Ads for conversion to Judaism classes may qualify for a subsidy. The National Center to Encourage Judaism will provide subsidies for advertisements concerning such classes. The ads must be in the secular, non-Jewish press. The subsidy will provide half the cost of one or more ads, up to a total of $300 per year. A bonus will be given for particularly original and catchy ads. To apply for the subsidy, the congregation or organization sponsoring the conversion class needs to send a copy of the ad or ads, a receipt for payment, and a statement of how many converts the organization welcomed into Judaism during the previous year. For further information, call (301) 593-2319. All materials should be submitted to:

National Center to Encourage Judaism
Box 651
Silver Spring, MD 20918

10. *Prepare brochures, posters, flyers, letters to the editor, and op-ed articles.*

There are other forms of writing that can be done for publicity, including brochures, posters, flyers, letters to the editor, and op-ed articles.

A. Relatively cheap threefold pamphlets can be used to explain the conversion class. The benefit of pamphlets is that they can contain all the needed information, are easy to read, and can be folded and carried in a pocket, wallet, or purse. If a pamphlet is used, the cover headline should stand out. Some eye-catching visual design should be used on the cover.

B. All materials, especially posters, need to be proofread very carefully for mistakes. Obviously on the poster the message needs to be brief, direct, and attractively laid out. Volunteer professional help would be very useful.

C. Flyers should be eye-catching, with some key words at the top in large print to attract readers. Flyers on different-colored paper can often be effective.

D. Almost all newspapers have a "Letters to the Editor" section. This section is one of the most popular with readers. Although not all letters are printed, brief and interesting letters often are. A letter about the conversion course as valuable for the community is appropriate.

E. Many newspapers set aside the page opposite the editorial page for opinion articles. An op-ed article about the course can be submitted. It will be especially valuable if it is written by a well-known member of the community.

11. *Deliver flyers and pamphlets.*

Deliver flyers and pamphlets to local Jewish institutions such as Jewish Community Centers, Y's, Jewish schools, and Jewish Community Councils as well as all organizations that have agreed to distribute them. Deliver flyers and pamphlets to local colleges with Jewish-oriented courses, asking an instructor of such courses to announce the course and post the flyer. Also deliver flyers to appropriate public institutions such as libraries and museums and ask if the flyers can be put on bulletin boards and placed in public areas for distribution.

12. Put up posters.

Place posters in all stores and locations that allow you to do so. Use the list of stores compiled for your mailing and contact list. If posters are not available, flyers can be substituted.

13. Send news releases and flyers.

Send your news releases and flyers to your entire mailing and contact list. Although this may be very early for a newspaper, you will need enough lead time to attract students. The usual deadlines are 2 to 3 weeks for a story, 1 week for a news event, and 2 weeks for a calendar listing.

14. Contact reporters for a story.

Newspaper, radio, and television reporters can be called directly about a week after the news releases have been sent to them. If possible, contact the religion reporters at both Jewish and secular papers and suggest a story. If you don't know who covers religion, call the paper and ask. Be prepared to fax or re-send all materials after this follow-up. Radio interviews over the telephone ("actualities") are effective, as are stories taped or recorded on location or in the studio. For radio and tv, contact the news director.

15. Contact graduates of conversion classes.

If you have had previous Introduction to Judaism classes, contact graduates of those classes and ask if they know anyone interested in taking the course.

16. Send op-ed pieces to newspapers.

These can appear as soon as 7 to 10 days after being submitted if they are selected for publication.

17. Send Public Service Announcements.

18. Place advertisements.

Four Weeks before the Course:

19. Send out speakers to discuss the class.

Speakers can volunteer to talk about the course at local Jewish congregations and organizations, public libraries, adult education classes, and so on.

20. Write letters to the editor.

21. Do follow-up calls.

Do follow-up calls to publications, reporters, and others on your mailing list. Try especially to get stories in local media.

Two Weeks before the Course:

22. Ask those who sign up for the course if they know people who would like to learn about the course and send a flyer to them.

23. Call all those who have inquired about the course but have not yet enrolled to determine if they wish to do so.

Taken together, all these activities will attract and retain an increasing number of students for the conversion to Judaism class.

Q. How do I start a discussion group for converts?

Epstein. I've discussed this idea in various parts of the book. Let me just say in this section that it is vital to become involved starting or working with a *keruv* group as described earlier or a specific discussion group only for those who have converted. In either case, it is very valuable for such groups to exist. Speak with a rabbi, write a brief article about your experiences for your synagogue bulletin or local secular and Jewish papers looking for people with similar experiences, talk to local Jewish communal workers such as at Jewish Community Centers to see if they know people who could join such groups.

Q. Do I have a special role to play in the Jewish community?

Epstein. I think converts have a very special role. You are in a unique position to explain Judaism to Gentile family members and friends and others who themselves might be interested in joining the Jewish people. I like to use the concept of converts being the best Ambassadors of Judaism, people who are able to interpret Judaism in areas outside itself.

Most of all, I encourage converts to Judaism who wish to do so to speak out about their experiences and write about them. The Jewish community, indeed the entire community, needs to hear significant stories of searches for meaning, searches that end in finding the treasure that is Judaism.

Index

About the Author

Lawrence J. Epstein is a Professor of English at a college in New York State. He is the author of *Samuel Goldwyn* (1981), *Zion's Call* (1984), *A Treasury of Jewish Anecdotes* (1989), *The Theory and Practice of Welcoming Converts to Judaism* (1992), *A Treasury of Jewish Inspirational Stories* (1993), and *Conversion to Judaism: A Guidebook* (1994). He also edited *Readings on Conversion to Judaism* (1995), and has written more than 100 articles, stories, and reviews on Jewish life that have appeared in major Jewish periodicals. Dr. Epstein has served as an advisor on the Middle East to two members of the United States Congress. He is the founder of the Conversion to Judaism Home Page on the World Wide Web and the founder and President of the Conversion to Judaism Resource Center. Dr. Epstein is married, and he and his wife, Sharon, have four children.